25

Celebrate!

Parties for Kids

Celebrate!

Parties for Kids

Carol Cowden
and
Patsy Shawver

Westport Publishers, Inc.
Kansas City, Missouri

ISBN 0-933701-40-3

Library of Congress Cataloging-in-Publication Data

Cowden, Carol, 1947–
    Celebrate! : parties for kids / Carol Cowden and Patsy
Shawver.
       p.   cm.
    ISBN 0-933701-40-3 :
    1. Children's parties.   I. Shawver, Patsy, 1947–   . : II.
Title.
  GV1205.C69 1989
  793.2'1—dc20   89-16450
                                                  CIP

J

1-8-90

Designed by Red Line Design Consultants
Some illustrations adapted from earlier work
of Rudy Garcia

Dedicated to the world's most patient children—Jennifer, John, Erin, and Brian—and to the hope that someday they will forget being late to soccer practice or not having clean socks for school and remember only the wonderful times shared with their families.

Table of Contents

Preface

Every adult can recall special moments of childhood that were characterized by happiness, love, and closeness with friends and family. These moments might have been a birthday, Christmas, or a party with friends. This book is created with the hope that we may help you stage such happy memories for your little ones, memories they will be able to someday share with their own children. Time goes so quickly—we don't ever want to look back and say, "Gee, I wish we'd taken time for that" or "Wouldn't that have been a fun thing to do?" The time is now——so let's celebrate!

Before You Begin . . .

Don't feel you must work for weeks making handmade invitations, favors, and special treats in order to hold a successful party. This book provides ideas for both those who enjoy creating their own props and those who want to use the wonderful selection at local card and party shops. Either way, with proper planning, your guests will have a delightful time. Plan your gathering in a way that best suits you—for you must enjoy yourself, too.

Below are some suggestions for making your event go smoothly:

1. Encourage your child's participation in every facet of the party.

2. Invite only the number of children you feel is appropriate. Also consider the size and nature of the party site. (For example, think long and hard before inviting 25 three-year-olds to drink red punch on your living room carpet!)

3. Invitations may be mailed, hand-delivered, or extended by telephone, but be sure to give your guests ample time to prepare for your party. Hand-deliveries may be made at school when the whole class is invited; otherwise, drop the invitations by your guests' homes. Telephone invitations are best extended from parent to parent to ensure accurate communication. Include all the necessary information, such as occasion, name, time, date, location, and phone number to which guests may respond.

4. To determine the length of your gathering, once again consider the age of the guests. Be sure to allow for travel time to and from the party location if it is to be held away from your home.

5. If there will be presents, make sure an adult supervises their opening so that each giver may be properly recognized. The process should move quickly so that guests' attention is not lost.

6. Gather game props, prizes, and favors beforehand. A laundry basket is one way to keep them handy and portable. It is a good idea to have a few extra prizes for unanticipated needs such as surprise guests, broken favors, and tie-breakers.

THERE'S ALWAYS A REASON TO CELEBRATE

JANUARY

3rd___Alaska became the 49th state in 1959. Make snow ice cream.

4th___Jakob Grimm, author and collector of fairy tales, was born in 1785. Invite children to dress as favorite fairy tale characters.

5th___Birthday of George Washington Carver, botanist, in 1864. Plant seeds.

6th___Poet Carl Sandburg was born in 1878. Suggest writing poems for teachers.

7th___Sherlock Holmes's birthday. Great day for a detective party!

9th___First human ascent in a balloon in America in 1793. Good excuse for a balloon party.

10th___First meeting of the United Nations in 1946. Try an "Around the World" party.

11th___First milk delivery in glass bottles in 1878. Visit a dairy.

12th___First steamboat built in 1812. Take a ride on a riverboat.

13th___Charles Perrault, French author of *Cinderella* and *Sleeping Beauty*, was born in 1628. Have a costume ball!

16th___Andre Michelin, industrialist and owner of first factories for mass production of rubber tires, was born in France in 1853. Go tubing in the snow.

17th___Benjamin Franklin was born in 1706. Try out some fun science experiments at a party for young inventors.

18th___Birthdate of A. A. Milne in 1882. Create a party around a Winnie the Pooh theme.

19th___Edgar Allen Poe was born in 1809. Tell scary stories in the dark.

24th___Gold was discovered at Sutter's Mill, California, in 1848. A treasure hunt would be fun on this day!

25th___Soviets released close-up pictures of Venus taken by the Venus 7 spacecraft. Find Venus in the night sky.

26th___Australia Day celebrates the landing of the first settlers at Sydney. Since Australia is the "Land Down Under," how about a backwards party?

27th___Lewis Carroll, author of *Alice in Wonderland*, was born in 1832. Have a tea party.

29th___Kansas Day! Kansas became a state in 1861. Rent the video "Wizard of Oz."

30th___First jazz recording by the Original Dixieland Jazz Band in New Jersey in 1917. Make a banjo out of a shoe box and rubber bands and have a jam session.

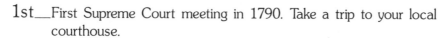

THERE'S ALWAYS A REASON TO CELEBRATE

FEBRUARY

1st—First Supreme Court meeting in 1790. Take a trip to your local courthouse.

2nd—Groundhog Day. Organize a game of shadow tag.

4th—Charles A. Lindbergh was born in 1902. Hold a paper airplane flying contest.

6th—Birthday of Babe Ruth in 1895. Play indoor baseball with a balloon and rolled up paper.

8th—Birthdate of Jules Verne, French writer of *Around the World in Eighty Days,* in 1828. Plan your own trip around the world. What countries would you visit?

10th—The first singing telegram was delivered in 1933. Create a singing telegram for a friend.

11th—Thomas Edison, inventor, was born in 1847. Give a prize for an invention that would make life easier at your house.

14th—Valentine's Day. Have a good time with the "Have a Heart" party.

15th—Italian astronomer, Galileo, was born in 1564. Visit the planetarium.

16th—Ulysses S. Grant forced the surrender of Confederate troops at Ft. Donelson in 1862. Take a tour of Civil War battlefields near you.

17th—The first sardine was canned in 1876. Have a contest to see how many people can fit into a box, small car, etc.

19th—Thomas Edison patented the phonograph in 1878. Invite friends over and ask them to bring their favorite records.

20th—The U.S. Mail Service was established in 1792. Have a letter-writing party.

22nd—Popcorn was introduced to the colonists in 1630. Children could come over after school to watch movies and pop popcorn.

23rd—George Frederick Handel, German-English composer, was born in 1685. Listen to a recording of the Hallelujah Chorus from the "Messiah." Count the "hallelujahs."

25th—Pierre Auguste Renoir, French Impressionist painter, was born in 1841. Visit an art museum and find the Renoirs.

26th—Birthdate of William Cody (Buffalo Bill), American scout, in 1846. Seek out a buffalo herd in a nature preserve near you.

27th—Henry Wadsworth Longfellow, poet who wrote "Hiawatha," was born in 1807. Make an Indian drum from a coffee can and a piece of vinyl.

28th—Charles Blondin, tightrope walker who crossed Niagara Falls many times, was born in France in 1824. Plan a neighborhood circus.

29th—Leap Year! Have girls ask a boy over for a snack!

THERE'S ALWAYS A REASON TO CELEBRATE

1st___First United States Bank established in 1780. Invite friends or neighbors in for a "Monopoly" tournament.

2nd___First around-the-world non-stop airplane flight in 1949. Have a paper airplane party. Contest could include longest flight, biggest, smallest, or most creative design.

4th___Dr. Suess was born in 1904. Invite friends to dress as their favorite Dr. Suess character.

7th___Luther Burbank, American horticulturist, was born in 1849. Have a peanut party!

8th___New York passed the first dog licensing law. Have a neighborhood pet show.

12th___First parachute jump in 1912. Make handkerchief and clothespin parachutes. Drop them from a safe, high place to see whose lands the quickest.

14th___First transatlantic broadcast in 1925. Tour a local radio station.

15th___The "Ides of March" on which Julius Caesar was assassinated in 44 B.C. Give each guest a sheet to see who can make the most creative toga.

17th___St. Patrick's Day. Throw a "shamrock shenanigan" party. Wear green and make green food.

22nd___Patrick Henry delivered his "Give Me Liberty or Give Me Death" speech in 1775. Have an old-fashioned patriotic celebration. Wear red, white, and blue.

23rd___Roger Bannister, the first man to run a mile in less than four minutes, was born in 1939. Have an "Olympics" party!

24th___Harry Houdini, American magician, was born in 1874. Host a neighborhood magic show.

25th___Gutzon Borglum, American sculptor who created faces on Mt. Rushmore, was born in 1871. Have a soap-carving contest, using heavy-duty plastic knives.

27th___First coast-to-coast television broadcast was made in 1955. Invite friends to get together dressed as their favorite television characters.

31st___The Eiffel Tower was completed in 1889. Try an "Around the World" party!

THERE'S ALWAYS A REASON TO CELEBRATE

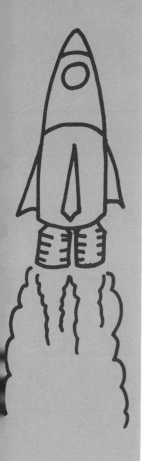

1st___April Fool's Day. Try the "Lid Off a Daffodil" party.

2nd___Hans Christian Andersen, Danish writer and collector of fairy tales, was born in 1805. Pantomime favorite fairy tales.

3rd___Pony Express began in 1860. Ride horses at local stables.

4th___Pocahontas married John Rolfe in 1614. Find out if you have an Indian museum or burial ground in your area and visit it.

6th___Admiral Robert Perry and four Eskimos discovered the North Pole in 1909. Build an igloo of sugar cubes.

7th___The only camel race ever held in the United States occurred in 1864 in Sacramento, California. Find a sandbox or nearby beach and build sand castles.

8th___Sonja Henie, world champion ice skater, was born in 1913. Visit a nearby indoor ice skating rink.

10th___Walter Hurst patented the safety pin in 1897. Using assorted boxes, glue, tape, rubber bands, cardboard tubes, and paint, who can design the best new invention?

12th___Soviet Yuri Gagarin orbited the earth in 1961. Design a "space ship" with an orange or apple, toothpicks, grapes, berries, and other fruits. Eat your creation!

13th___Birthdate of the man who invented the "dime store," Frank W. Woolworth. Visit your local dime store.

18th___Paul Revere made his famous ride in 1775. No horse? Hold bicycle races.

20th___New York World's Fair opened in 1939. Stage a neighborhood carnival. Each family can design and man a game booth.

22nd___Arbor Day. Plant a tree! If you cannot plant a tree, try a seed, flower, or bush—inside or out.

23rd___William Shakespeare was born in 1564. Try a poetry writing contest.

26th___John James Audubon, American ornithologist and artist, was born in 1785. Take a nature walk. Take along a sketch pad and draw the most special birds you see along the way.

29th___Gideon Sundback patented the "separable fastener," forerunner to the zipper, in 1913. List how many things use a zipper.

APRIL

THERE'S ALWAYS A REASON TO CELEBRATE

MAY

1st____May Day. Deliver flowers to special friends.

2nd____Pranconi's Hippodrome (an amusement park seating 4,000) opened in New York in 1853 with chariot races and ostrich races. Create your own races with Big Wheels, bicycles, wheelbarrows, or wagons.

3rd____Beginning of three days of kite battles in Hamamatsu, Japan. Take friends in an open area to fly kites. Whose goes the highest? Whose stays up the longest?

4th____The Academy of Motion Picture Arts and Sciences was founded in 1927. Rent a classic movie with friends.

6th____The first postage stamp, the "penny black," was issued in England in 1840. Hold a stamp designing contest. What will you put on it? A person? An animal? A flower?

9th____Mother's Day became a public holiday in 1914. Pamper Mom by fixing breakfast or lunch.

15th____Donald Duncan, inventor of the yo-yo, died in 1971. Invite friends to bring yo-yos for an afternoon of fun.

16th____The first motion picture Oscars were awarded in 1929. See the "Birthday Bijou" party for "reel" movie fun!

17th____The first Kentucky Derby was held in 1875. Tour your local stables.

19th____The first performance of Ringling Brothers Circus took place in 1884. Put on a neighborhood circus.

21st____The first bicycles were imported from England to the United States in 1819. Take a family bicycle tour.

24th____Morse code was first sent over telegraph wire in 1844. Make up your own code and send a message to a friend.

25th____Babe Ruth was born in 1895. Attend a local baseball or softball game.

26th____The first steamship to cross the Atlantic, the USS Savannah, arrived in 1819. Make boats carved from "floatable soap." Scoop out a hole in the center. Insert a popsicle stick and paper sail into the hole with clay. Hold a race at a nearby creek or pond.

27th____Amelia Bloomer, designer of the "bloomer," was born in 1818. Have a dress-up party.

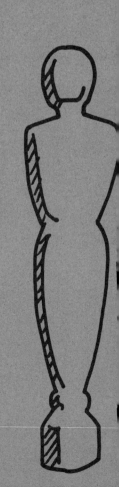

3rd___The last great auk was captured in 1844. Auks were last seen in the wild in 1853. Visit the zoo.

4th___Henry Ford test-drove the first Ford car around Detroit in 1896. Visit an automobile assembly plant or invite a friend over to help build a model.

6th___The first drive-in movie opened in Camden, New Jersey, in 1933. Visit a local drive-in movie.

8th___Ice cream was first advertised and sold in America in 1786. Have a neighborhood ice cream making contest.

12th___Baseball was reputedly invented in 1839 by Abner Doubleday. Have a baseball card trading party.

13th___Basil Rathbone was born in 1892. Show a video of an old scary movie.

14th___Flag Day. Organize a neighborhood parade.

16th___Ben Franklin proved lightning was a form of electricity in 1752. Organize a kite-flying expedition.

17th___The first Republican convention was held in 1856. Go to the zoo to ride the elephant.

20th___Ed Sullivan's television variety show made its debut in 1948. Hold a neighborhood talent show.

22nd___Joe Louis became the world heavyweight boxing champion in 1937, a title he held until 1949 when he retired. Hold a supervised pillow fight.

24th___Trees have finished their annual growth by now. Hold a contest to discover the best "climbing" tree in the neighborhood.

25th___The United Nations began in 1945. Invite friends over for an international dinner.

26th___Final day of the National Marble Tourney in Wildwood, New Jersey, in 1970. Hold a marble-shooting contest.

28th___To help Pennsylvania farmers dispose of an egg surplus, slot machines dispensing hard-boiled eggs for a nickel each were installed in cafes and taverns across the state in 1938. Easter season is not the only time for an egg hunt. Hard boil eggs and hide them in the yard.

JUNE

THERE'S ALWAYS A REASON TO CELEBRATE

JULY

1st___Anniversary of the first American postage stamp. Write a letter to a pen pal.

3rd___The start of "The Potato War" over the Bavarian throne occurred in 1805. Invite friends over to decorate a potato. Use raw potatoes, tooth-picks, peas, cheese cubes, olives, etc.

4th___Tom Sawyer Day in Hannibal, Missouri. Have a fence-painting race, using paint brushes and water.

6th___The first all-talking picture, "Lights of New York," opened in New York in 1928. Write and produce a movie with a video camera.

8th___The first Ziegfeld Follies opened in 1907. Choreograph your own dance production with friends. How about a water ballet?

9th___The first rhinoceros born in captivity was born in Ireland in 1969. Take a picnic to your local zoo.

11th___United States frogmen swam the English Channel underwater in 18 hours. Try "The Big Splash" party.

13th___The first television broadcast was aired in 1930. Have a party where guests dress up as favorite TV characters.

14th___Bastille Day became a French national holiday in 1880. Serve French food for lunch or dinner. Croissants? Crepes? Omelets? French fries?

20th___Neil Armstrong landed on the moon in 1969. Visit the local planetarium.

23rd___The ice cream cone was invented in 1904. Invite the neighbors for homemade ice cream.

28th___An egg was fried on the steps of the United States Capitol in 1928. Have an omelet party. Guests can choose what goodies to put into their omelets.

29th___A total eclipse of the sun occurred in 1878. Look through a kaleido-scope and draw what you see inside.

30th___"In God We Trust" officially became the United States motto in 1956. Have a penny-stacking contest. Who can build the highest stack without toppling it over?

31st___The saxophone, invented by Adolphe Sax, a Belgian musical instrument maker, was officially introduced to the military band of the French army. Make kazoos by poking two or three holes in the side of a cardboard tube, then wrapping it in waxed paper with a rubber band at one end. Hum into the open end for a kazoo sound.

THERE'S ALWAYS A REASON TO CELEBRATE

August is National Sandwich Month. Make a five-foot long submarine sandwich and share it with lots of friends!

The first week is National Clown Week. Throw a circus party and ask friends to dress up as clowns.

1st__Yves St. Laurent, fashion designer, was born in 1936. Put on a neighborhood fashion show.

5th__Annual magic convention was held at Colon, Michigan, in 1972. Put on a magic show. Find a book in the library for great tricks.

7th__Third Annual Pea Harvest was held at Palmer, Alaska, in 1970. Plan a dinner for the family, choosing all green foods (peas, green jello, olives, salad, etc.).

8th__Watermelon Festival was held at Rush Springs, Oklahoma, in 1970. Hold a seed-spitting contest. Prizes could be for best arch, farthest, best two out of three, etc.

12th__First patent was issued for an accordion in the United States in 1856. Make homemade instruments out of boxes and rubber bands. Staple two paper plates together with dried beans inside for great tambourine; put rubber piece from inner tube over the end of a coffee can to make a drum. Then form a neighborhood band.

13th__First annual convention of mailmen was held in 1890. Leave a surprise treat for your mailman.

14th__John Ringling North, circus showman, was born in 1903. Put on a neighborhood circus—tame the "wild dogs," do acrobatics, sell popcorn.

15th__Festival of Mountain Guides was held at Chamonix, France, started in 1971. Take an exploratory expedition into a nearby wooded area if you have one.

18th__First unassisted triple play in baseball was made by Harry O'Hagan in 1902. Go to a baseball game or organize one among friends.

21st__Hawaii became a state in 1959. Have a luau with everyone dressed in grass skirts and brightly colored shirts.

22nd__Yacht America won England's major sailboat race, which became the America's Cup sailing challenges in 1851. Race toy boats in a shallow creek.

23rd__World's tallest totem pole dedicated at Kake, Alaska, in 1969. Make a totem pole out of boxes and cans.

28th__First radio commercial was broadcast in 1922. Make up a radio program and present it to the neighbors.

29th__In 1957, Senator Strom Thurmond of South Carolina set a senate filibuster record of 24 hours 18 minutes over the civil rights bill, which passed anyway. Check the *Guinness Book of World Records* to see what kind of record you might be able to set (such as who can hold their breath the longest).

30th__Baltimore and Ohio Railroad ran its first locomotive, the "Tom Thumb," by steam in 1830. Take a train ride.

THERE'S ALWAYS A REASON TO CELEBRATE

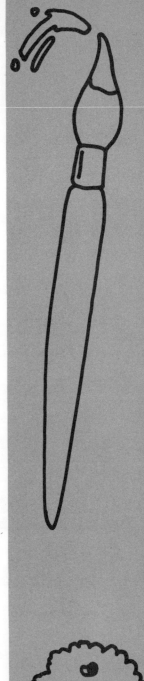

2nd__Cleveland Amory, author-critic, was born in 1917. Organize a movie expedition and write your own reviews of the film.

3rd__Louis Sullivan, architect credited with inventing the skyscraper, was born. Go to the top of a tall building.

7th__Grandma Moses was born in 1860. Hold a neighborhood art festival.

9th__American Bowling Congress was organized in 1895. Go bowling.

10th__Sewing machine was patented in 1846. Make a coat for your dog or cat.

13th__Milton S. Hershey, candy-maker, was born in 1857. Make fudge.

14th__In 1814 Frances Scott Key wrote the words to the "Star Spangled Banner." Hold a contest to write a new national anthem and give lots of prizes.

16th__Mexico's Independence Day. Break open a piñata.

19th__Mickey Mouse made his debut in 1928 in "Steamboat Willie." Show cartoons and wear mouse ears.

21st__First daily newspaper was published in 1784. Write an issue of a neighborhood paper.

23rd__In 1939, a time capsule was buried in Flushing Meadow Park, New York, to be opened in 6939. Plant your own time capsule with all sorts of fun things and decide when you want to have it opened.

24th__Babe Ruth made his last appearance with the New York Yankees in 1934. Have a hitting contest and serve Baby Ruth candy bars.

26th__In 1774, Johnny Appleseed was born. Plant a tree, apple or otherwise.

28th__Confucius's birthday was celebrated on Taiwan in 1970. Make up funny Confucius sayings.

THERE'S ALWAYS A REASON TO CELEBRATE

3rd__Child Health Day. Take a tour of a hospital.

4th__Sputnik I was launched in 1957 by the Soviet Union. Have a party where guests dress up as creatures from outer space.

5th__In 1964, Janice Pepper married Francis Salt in England. Think of some other silly combinations, such as Harold S. P. Getty marrying Marian Sauce.

7th__Fire Prevention Week. Invite friends over to make posters on the subject.

9th__The Fingerprint Society (International Association for Criminal Identification) was founded in 1915. Create thumbprint animals.

10th__Olympic Games opened in Tokyo in 1964. Have an Olympics party.

14th__First baby show in the United States was held in Ohio in 1854. Get out your old baby pictures and have friends bring theirs over, too.

15th__National Poetry Day. Use a list of silly words to make into a rhyme.

16th__Noah Webster was born. Find ten unfamiliar words in the dictionary.

19th__First general court held at Boston, Massachusetts, in 1630. Hold a mock trial for something silly such as the dog getting into the trash or for someone forgetting to put the lid on the toothpaste.

21st__Thomas Edison invented the light bulb. Think up some new, wonderful invention that will help you clean your room or do your homework for you.

23rd__Each year the swallows leave Capistrano on this day. Find out how many kinds of birds live in your yard. Get a book at the library and try to identify them.

24th__Sarah J. B. Hale, who composed "Mary Had a Little Lamb," was born in 1788. Visit a petting zoo.

26th__Joseph Hansom, cab inventor, was born in 1881. Take a cab ride.

29th__National Children's Book Week. Start a reading contest, with rewards for reading a designated number of pages by a certain date.

THERE'S ALWAYS A REASON TO CELEBRATE

NOVEMBER

2nd___Daniel Boone was born in 1734. Go camping.

3rd___First automobile show opened in New York City in 1900. Hold a race of toy cars on a ramp made out of old wood.

5th___Crossword puzzles first appeared in book form in 1924. Try a crossword puzzle contest.

8th___First circulating library established in Philadelphia in 1731. Tour a library and see all it has to offer in addition to books.

12th___Jules Leotard, the man on the flying trapeze, was introduced at a Paris circus in 1859. Have a trick contest on a swing set.

13th___In 1850 Robert Louis Stevenson was born. Have a pirate party and go on a treasure hunt.

14th___*Moby Dick* was published by Herman Melville in 1851. Visit a pet store and look at all the remarkable types of fish.

15th___Zebulon Pike discovered Pike's Peak in 1806. Go on a hike.

21st___Thomas Edison invented the phonograph in 1877. Visit a recording studio with some friends and record a tape.

23rd___Boris Karloff was born in 1887. Host a monster party complete with costumes and make-up. Tell ghost stories.

25th___In 1834, a three-course meal could be obtained at Delmonico's in New York for 12¢. Go to the grocery store with a couple of friends and see if you can buy *anything* for 12¢.

26th___Charles Schultz, creator of the comic strip "Peanuts," was born in 1922. Invite everyone for a party and have them dress as their favorite cartoon character.

27th___David Merrick, theatrical producer, was born in 1912. Help your children put on a play.

28th___Thanksgiving was first observed in the United States in 1623. Make some sort of Thanksgiving tray favors, little turkeys out of pine cones with gum drops stuck on for feathers, etc., and deliver them to a nursing home.

30th___Mark Twain was born in 1835. Start reading as a family the antics of Tom Sawyer and Huckleberry Finn.

THERE'S ALWAYS A REASON TO CELEBRATE

1st___First telephone was installed at the White House in 1878. Make a telephone by attaching two cans with a long string.

2nd___George Washington nicknamed New York the "Empire State" in 1784. Find out other state nicknames and have a contest to see who knows the most.

3rd___Planet Uranus was discovered in 1714 by John Flamsteed. Try to memorize all of the planets and their location from the sun.

5th___Walt Disney was born in 1901. Dress as a Disney character.

9th___Emmett Kelly, a famous clown, was born in 1898. Dress up like clowns, make-up and all.

10th___Pancake festivals are held at Hazelton and Wilkes-Barre, Pennsylvania. Have breakfast in bed and serve pancakes, of course.

11th___Laughing gas was first used in 1844 for a tooth extraction. Share jokes.

15th___J. Paul Getty, millionaire, was born in 1892. Start a collection of a million of something—paper clips, bottle caps, pennies, or whatever. What does a million look like?

16th___Ludwig van Beethoven's birthday. Make your own musical instruments and have a concert.

17th___The Wright brothers made the first successful air flight at Kitty Hawk, North Carolina, in 1903. Visit an airport and take a tour.

22nd___U.S. Golf Association formed in 1894. Hold a family peanut golf tournament.

23rd___"The Night Before Christmas" was first published in 1823. Read this wonderful poem.

25th___Robert Ripley, creator of *Ripley's Believe It or Not*, was born in 1893. Get a copy of this fascinating book and share some of the incredible facts.

27th___Howdy Doody television show first aired in 1947. Have a puppet show.

28th___W. F. Semple received the first patent for chewing gum in 1869. Have a bubble blowing contest.

31st___"Touch a Pig for Luck" day in Austria. Find out about all sorts of lucky superstitions.

INVITATIONS

SUPER SLEUTH

Begin the intrigue by writing the invitation backwards so it can be read when held up to a mirror.

PLACE:
TIME:
Date:

Children of all ages love adventure. The Super Sleuth detective party offers mystery, intrigue, and outrageous fun.

Write party information on an inflated balloon, then deflate and tuck into an envelope. Guest must blow up balloon to read the message.

Write information in invisible ink with instructions for decoding message attached.

Code the message and attach instructions for deciphering.

- *Puzzle Race:* Give each child a puzzle you have made by cutting a construction paper shape into puzzle pieces. Pieces may be put in an envelope or paper-clipped together. At the signal, children begin assembling puzzle. First to complete it wins.

- *Guesstimation:* Have children guess the number of peanuts or candies in a jar. This is especially good while waiting for all the guests to arrive, or if you run out of things to do before time is up. Child closest to the correct number wins jar.

- *Missing Masterpiece:* As the children arrive at the party, have each draw a picture of something. Do not have them sign their work. A little later in the party, announce that some missing masterpieces have been discovered. Children are to try to identify who drew each masterpiece.

- *Memory Teaser:* Display a tray of common items (comb, scissors, pencil, ruler, eraser, spoon, etc.) and give children sixty seconds to study it. Then cover tray with a towel and give them five minutes to write down everything they can remember. Child with the most items on his list wins.

- *Identify the Flavor:* Give children gourmet jelly beans of various flavors and see if they can identify each taste. This also can be done with objects to feel or smell. Or tape record sounds, such as running water, toilet flushing, telephone ringing, alarm clock buzzing, etc. Children can be blindfolded and given objects to identify by touching, such as sponge, cold spaghetti, grapes, or little pencil shavings.

INVISIBLE INK

ENTERTAINMENT

REFRESHMENTS

Magnifying Glass Cake—
Bake one layer in round pan
and one in bread pan. Place
together as illustrated in
picture. Frost with chocolate,
except center of round layer
which should be frosted with
white icing.

Have children hunt for the
refreshments (wrapped candies,
cupcakes, condiments for
sundaes) by hiding them
around the house or outdoors.
Make sugar cookies in shape
of a question mark. Cut
pattern from heavy paper,
place on top of rolled cookie
dough, and cut around shape
with knife.

Mystery Punch—Mix together
several fruit flavored beverages
and have the children guess
what fruit flavors are in
the punch.

No good detective should
be without:

Whistle lollipops
Invisible ink
Magnifying glasses
Paperback mysteries
Toy handcuffs
Blank puzzles

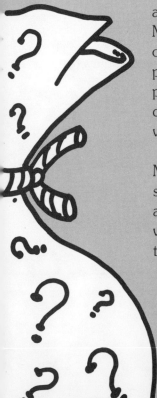

FAVORS

Gather a posse of your child's favorite friends and step back into the Old West. The corral could be your own backyard or neighborhood park. Area stables for horseback riding or hayrides would be perfect. Have guests dress in cowboy clothes or supply inexpensive bandanas or cowboy hats as they arrive.

INVITATIONS

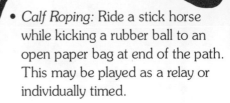

Roll up handmade invitations and tie with jute or rope.

Wrap your invitation in a bandana and tie with a rope. Guests could wear the bandana to the party.

- *Calf Roping:* Ride a stick horse while kicking a rubber ball to an open paper bag at end of the path. This may be played as a relay or individually timed.

- *Stock Hunt:* Hide equal number of plastic or paper horses and cows around the room. Assign a captain for each of two teams. When one teammate from the horse crew finds a horse, he "whinnies" and stays there until his captain comes and finds the horse. Team looking for cows "moos" upon finding cows. Captain keeps animals. Team with the most animals wins.

- *Memory Game:* See "Games" in Resource Section. Use cowboy items on tray (plastic cowboys or Indians, sheriff's badge, toy gun, rope, etc.).

- *Sweep out the Barn:* Furnish each of two teams with a broom and a sock rolled into a ball. First player on each team sweeps sock to designated point and then back to next player, who repeats action. Play continues until one team completes the course.

- *Suitcase Game:* See "Games" in Resource Section. Adapt by using cowboy clothes in suitcase.

ENTERTAINMENT

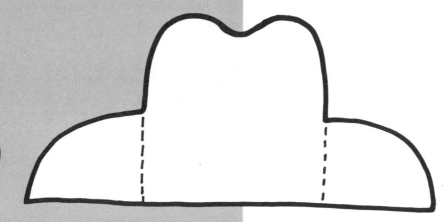

Circle your wagons and round up the gang for chuckwagon lunch. Try these menu ideas:

Pigs-in-a-Blanket—Place a cheese slice inside a hot dog slit lengthwise, wrap with canned biscuit dough, and bake at 375 degrees until dough is lightly browned.

Hamburgers, hot dogs, barbecued beef
Baked beans
Coleslaw
Shoestring potatoes
Root beer

Try making a cowboy hat cake. Bake cake in one square and one round pan. Cut a small dip in top of square cake for top of hat. Remove a 3-inch strip from center of round cake and place remaining pieces on either side of square for brim. Frost as desired.

Sheriff's badges can be purchased at variety stores or can be cut from heavy paper and covered with foil.

Bandanas can be purchased inexpensively at discount and variety stores.

Take instant pictures of each child on a wagon or a horse, put in a cardboard frame, and encircle with rope or jute.

Cookies in the shape of a star can be decorated with child's name in icing.

Plastic cowboys, Indians, and horses can be purchased at most discount and toy stores.

FAVORS

BIRTHDAY BIJOU

If taking a large group of children to the movies does not fit into your plans, then bring the movie home. Your living room or family room can be the setting for a terrific, entertaining afternoon in all kinds of weather.

INVITATIONS

Design your own "marquee." Fold a 4 x 10-inch sheet of blue paper in half to make a 4 x 5-inch folded card. Decorate all four edges of the front with gold stars or dots to resemble marquee lights. In the center of the front write in gold or silver paint pen your child's name followed by "Birthday Bijou." Party information can be included inside on a ticket made from paper of another color.

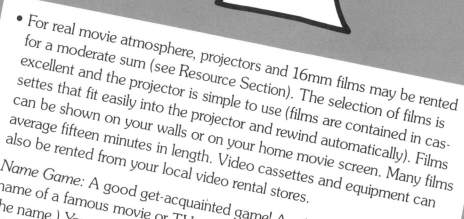

- For real movie atmosphere, projectors and 16mm films may be rented for a moderate sum (see Resource Section). The selection of films is excellent and the projector is simple to use (films are contained in cassettes that fit easily into the projector and rewind automatically). Films can be shown on your walls or on your home movie screen. Many films average fifteen minutes in length. Video cassettes and equipment can also be rented from your local video rental stores.

- *Name Game:* A good get-acquainted game! As children enter, pin the name of a famous movie or TV star on their backs. (They must not see the name.) You must be careful to choose names they will recognize. Children ask each other questions to discover their famous identity, but only questions that can be answered "yes" or "no." First to guess who he or she is wins. Some examples of famous characters children might enjoy are Miss Piggy, Mickey Mouse, E.T., Big Bird, or ALF.

- *Charades:* A classic.

- *Tracing Stars:* Give each child a pencil, sheet of paper, and a cardboard star shape. The one to trace the largest number of star shapes on his own paper without overlapping wins.

- *Categories:* Give every child a pencil and a copy of the chart on the next page. Fill in the left column with categories such as Male TV Star, Female TV Star, Male Movie Star, and Female Movie Star. The first child to complete the chart by filling in the blanks with stars whose last names begin with the letters at the top wins.

ENTERTAINMENT

REFRESHMENTS

Star Cake—Cut star shape from large sheet cake or use star-shaped baking pan available from the cake decorating center at your local department store. Ice with yellow icing.

Clapstick Cake—Ice sheet cake with white icing and decorate as illustrated with chocolate tube icing.

More good movie food:

Popcorn and cola
G.O.R.P. (see Resource Section)
Licorice

Make star-shaped bean bags from yellow felt.

Sunglasses are a must for every movie star.

Offer movie posters or TV or movie trading cards.

"Star" cookie baked on a stick can be decorated with child's name, wrapped in plastic, and tied with yarn. Directions for baking cookies on a stick can be found in the Resource Section.

FAVORS

This is a great summertime activity for your neighborhood pool. Some pools even let you rent the whole area after hours. During cooler weather, check local motels to see if their indoor pools are available.

Some motels will allow small groups to use the pool if an adult rents a room for the day. The room can be used for changing clothes, snacking, and game playing. Make sure guests know how to swim, are comfortable in the water, and that they understand safety rules. With younger children, make sure you have plenty of adult help.

THE BIG SPLASH

From colored paper, cut shapes that suggest water un—fish, surf board, goggles, bubbles, or a snorkel. Write necessary facts about the party on the front.

Write message on an inexpensive beach ball and hand deliver.

- These games are appropriate for children who are comfortable in the water.

- *Water Races:* Set up relay teams and let the children race from one spot to another doing whatever stroke they do best. Have children race running through shallow water, hopping backwards, walking on their hands, or walking on all fours. Raft or inner tube races make a splash.

- *Bottle Brigade:* Form two teams of equal numbers. One brave member of each team lies on the ground and holds an empty plastic 2-liter bottle on his forehead. Other team members fill small cups from a bucket of water and form a "bottle brigade" line. Each person runs up and pours the water from the cup into the bottle, then runs back and the next team member goes. Continue until one team's bottle is filled.
  Variation: With same two teams, last child puts empty bottle in his pocket. Each team member has a styrofoam cup. The first child fills his up from a bucket of water and pours it into the next teammate's cup. This continues until last child with cup pours the water into the empty bottle in his friend's pocket. Play continues until a bottle is full.

- *Water Ballet:* Let the children choreograph a ballet in the pool. It could be silly or serious.

- *Water Balloon Toss:* The children form two lines facing each other. Give all children on one side balloons filled with water. Each carefully tosses the balloon to his partner immediately across. After each toss, they each take a step away from their partners, increasing the distance between them. If a balloon drops and breaks, that team is out. The winning team is the one that gets the farthest away from each other while tossing the balloon.

- *Dive for Treasure:* The children dive for coins or small trinkets.

- *Swab the Deck:* This is a good game for younger children. Give each a clean paint brush and a can of water and let him "paint" to his heart's content on the pool deck or sidewalk. You might give awards for each masterpiece such as most original design, best brush strokes,

REFRESHMENTS

Any kind of treat for a hot day would be fun—popsicles, fruit salads, or a brown bag lunch packed for each child.

Snow Cones—Crush ice cubes made of orange juice or lemonade and serve in a paper cup.

Orange Frost (Recipe in Resource Section)

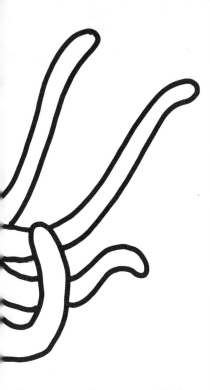

largest use of water, etc. Make sure everybody wins!

- *Move the Beach:* Divide into two teams. Give each team a container of sand and a spoon. Set a small bucket for each team at the end of the path. Each contestant carries a spoonful of sand to the bucket, dumps it into the pail, and runs back to the next teammate, handing him the spoon for his turn. The first team to fill the bucket wins. If this takes too long, award the prize to the team who has put the most sand into its bucket in a set amount of time.

- *Jump the Water:* The children jump over a stream of water running from a garden hose. The height of the stream can be raised with each round.

- *Balloon Sweep:* At a signal, each child rolls filled water balloons from start to finish by gently nudging with his feet. First to cross the finish line with balloon intact wins.

Ideas for summer fun favors include:

Water guns
Inexpensive
  sunglasses
Buckets and
  shovels
Sun visors
Bubbles and
  bubble wands
Beach ball
Umbrella hat
  (available from
  carnival supply
  stores)

FAVORS

OLYMPICS

INVITATIONS

Make medallions with construction paper containing party information. Attach a striped ribbon for more authenticity.

A good opportunity to include both boys and girls on the guest list. Ideally this party is best when it can be held outside, but many of the events can be adapted for a recreation room.

A drawing of the Olympic circles with a bit of information in each circle is also a good way to get the message across.

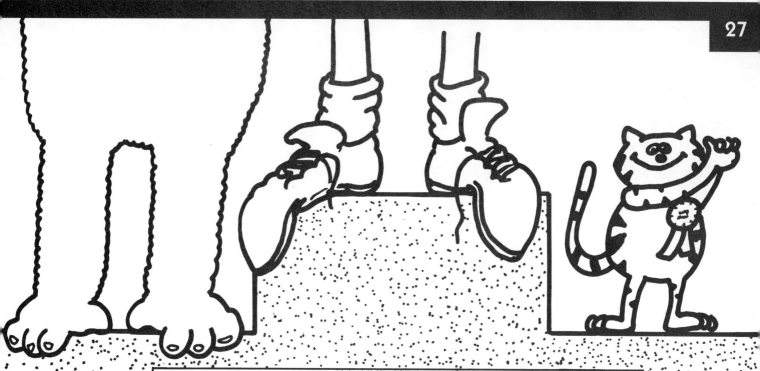

- *Javelin Throw:* Measure the distance each child throws a drinking straw.

- *Discus:* Measure the distance each child throws a frisbee.

- *Glove Practice:* Children put on cotton work gloves and attempt to pick up five sticks of gum on a flat surface. Child with the highest number in a set period wins.

- *Sharp Shooter:* With a stopwatch, time each child's attempts to extinguish a candle with a squirt gun from a given distance. Ideal for outside.

- *Ski Slope Shuffle:* Form two teams. First person on each team slips his feet into empty shoe boxes and shuffles to a given point and back. The next child in line puts his feet into the same empty boxes and shuffles off until all teammates are finished. First team to complete wins.

- *Super Sprints:* Races can be run backwards, hopping, balancing a frisbee on your head, singing, flapping arms, or carrying a glass of water.

- *Pitching Practice:* Have children throw metal washers into a muffin tin from a given distance. Child with the highest number of washers in a cup wins.

- *Steeple Chase:* Plan an obstacle course outside. Have funny things to do posted along the route (sing "Jingle Bells," run to the next tree backwards, say "girls are great" ten times, count to 100 by 5's, etc.).

- *Popcorn Pass:* Each relay team tries to fill a container with popcorn by carrying a spoonful at a time.

- *Jump Rope:* The child who rope jumps the most times in sixty seconds wins.

ENTERTAINMENT

REFRESHMENTS

Make sure to have healthy snacks such as Gatorade, fruits, or nuts. Red, white, and blue bomb pops would be fun.

Chocolate coins wrapped in gold foil make great medals when tied on a yarn ribbon and hung around the child's neck.

Inexpensive plastic trophies may be purchased at a variety store.

Purchase two-inch wide satin ribbon in red, white, or blue. Cut into six-inch pieces and attach small circles of paper on which are written such messages as "Good Job!", "Way to Go!", "Best Effort!", or other encouraging phrases. No need to designate first, second, or third place.

Gator Gum is a must for every athlete! Check your nearby sporting goods store.

FAVORS

Certainly the term "slumber" is not totally appropriate for this party, as it is rare that much slumbering goes on. But for an occasional special event, these are really fun!

To spice up the party, you might ask each guest to dress up as a favorite book or movie character. Or how about a "come-as-you-are" party? Call friends the week before early in the morning to invite them, and ask them to wear what they have on at that moment. You'll find an interesting variety of attire!

SWEET DREAMS

INVITATIONS

Write your message on purchased teddy bear stationery or a homemade paper teddy cut out of brown heavy paper.

How about enclosing your message in a plastic pop bottle and hand delivering?

• Have someone teach aerobics, jazz, or the latest dance craze. Call a local dance studio for the name of someone who might be available for a lesson. Or invite a big sister to teach cheerleading routines.

• Ask each guest to bring a favorite record or cassette, then have a dance contest with everyone winning some kind of prize (best dancer, most creative, most imaginative, fastest, slowest, funniest).

• If you have a videocassette recorder, show a popular movie and serve popcorn.

• Play charades. (See Resource Section.)

• If you are truly ambitious, give each girl an embroidery hoop with fabric stretched inside. Have them draw a simple design with a pencil and then teach them to embroider it. Naturally you wouldn't want to attempt this with a large number of children, but it is fun and gives the girls something to do while they stay up and "chat."

ENTERTAINMENT

REFRESHMENTS

Make pizza or tacos. Everyone will love helping! An individual pizza recipe is available in the Resource Section.

Make a jelly roll cake look like a sleeping bag by frosting it and tying a piece of string licorice around it.

Flower Pot Treats—Check the Resource Section for the recipe. This is a pretty dessert and yummy to eat!

To help your guests remember the party, give them:

Colorful combs
Barrettes
Fingernail polish
45 rpm records
Stickers
Small, inexpensive stuffed
   animals

FAVORS

AROUND THE WORLD

INVITATIONS

Send the guests a passport with the party facts written on the inside!

Write your party information on a drawing or cutout of a hot air balloon.

An Around the World party is a wonderful excuse to don a costume!

Invite guests to dress up representing a country of their choice or assign a country to each.

- *Break a Piñata:* These can be purchased inexpensively at carnival supply stores. Fill with candy and small favors and suspend from the ceiling. The children are blindfolded one at a time and then each takes a turn at striking the piñata with a broom handle. Keep taking turns until one child breaks the piñata open and candy spills out for all to gather.

- *Eiffel Tower:* Form two teams. Set up two short ladders at a given point and place several adults by ladders to ensure safety. Teammates run in order to ladder, climb to top and back down, then run back to next teammate, who continues. First team finished wins.

- *Kangaroo Hop:* Tie carpenter's aprons (available at local hardware stores or carnival supply stores) around first teammates in two relay lines. Place a stuffed animal in the pocket of each apron. Children hop to finish line and back, then remove apron and tie onto next teammate. First team to complete course wins.

- *Leaning Tower of Pisa:* Give a set of cardboard blocks (or empty tin cans) to each of two teams. At a signal, children stack blocks as high as they can. Highest tower that remains standing wins.

- *Mexican Hat Dance:* Children can dance around a straw hat to a recording of the "Mexican Hat Dance."

- *Pickup Sticks:* Form two teams. First child of each team picks up a grape with chopsticks and carries it to the finish line and back to the next teammate. Each child in line does the same until they all have carried the grape. First team done wins.

- *World Scramble:* Give each child a paper and pencil and a list of countries with letters scrambled. For example "ximcoe" would be Mexico, "risulataa" would be Australia, and "njapa" would be Japan. The first to unscramble all the countries correctly wins.

ENTERTAINMENT

REFRESHMENTS

A variety of international
snacks would be fun.
Choose from:

Hot dogs (USA)
Nachos or taco chips and
   cheese dip (Mexico)
Tropical fruit punch
   (Polynesia) or fresh fruit

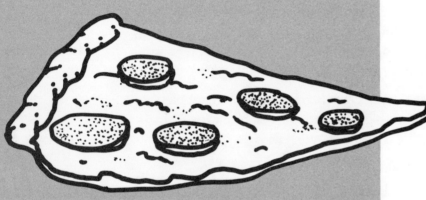

Croissants or beignets
   (France)
Chow mein noodles, fortune
   cookies, egg rolls (China)
Bratwurst (Germany)
Pizza or spaghetti (Italy)

Travel posters would be
great. Find a travel agent
to donate some.

Give inexpensive chopsticks
for the children to take home
and try.

International flags would be
an appropriate reminder of
the country which the child
represents.

Tiny Chinese parasols are
festive favors.

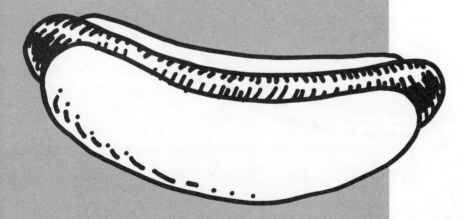

FAVORS

What's this, you say? Read it backwards and you'll see it's the same as forwards, just like this party—all turned around!

Sometimes being zany is just right for people of all ages. So throw good sense to the wind and "step on no pets." Hang your pictures backwards, have balloons hanging without air, face the chairs away from the table, place books on the shelves upside down, and put crepe paper streamers on the floor! Make it as crazy as you can!

INVITATIONS

Scramble the letters of each word of the invitation so the invitees will need to figure out the message. It might be a good idea to include the important information in proper form so you won't have guests showing up on the wrong day, at the wrong house, or wearing a dinosaur costume!

PLACE
DATE
TIME

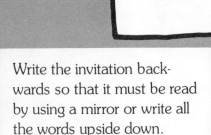

Write the invitation backwards so that it must be read by using a mirror or write all the words upside down.

Copy a fun picture from a book and hide the words of the invitation throughout. Don't make it too difficult or no one will know to come!

Create your message in pig latin—"easeplay omecay otay ymay artypay." How long has it been since you've talked that way?

- *Backward March!:* All the gues parade around the yard or hous in pure military style—except they're walking backwards. Ho about even having them put their clothes on backwards? This would be fun to catch on video and then show later on in the party.

- *Don't Pin the Ear on the Donke* Just like the traditional game, except the person the farthest from the target wins.

- *Hurray for Bob:* Give each gue paper and pencil. As you say "Go," everyone writes down th name of every other guest, but spelled backwards. The first person finished correctly wins.

- *Name Calling:* The party grou sits in a circle. "It" calls anothe guest's name, then the guest spells "its" name backwards quickly. If he does it correctly, he calls on someone to spell his name backwards. Sounds simple but when it gets going fast, it's challenging.

- *Oooh, What's That Smell?:* Fill a container with colored water, pass it around, and have all the guests guess what the liquid might be. It's actually plain water, but it's fun to hear what the imaginations come up with.

- *Throwing Your Money Around:* Divide players into two relay teams. The first player on each team runs up to a distant can, removes three pennies that are inside, and then on the way back to the line, drops them on the ground. The next player gathers up the pennies, puts them back in the can, and returns to the line. The third player repeats the actions of the first. Play continues until one team finishes.

- *Suckers Relay:* Players on two relay teams are each given a straw. The first person in line runs up to a pile of tissue paper squares, sucks up the top piece with a straw, and then returns to the line with it, the whole time keeping it on his straw. If it falls off, he has to pick it up with the straw and continue to the line. The play continues until all players have completed play.

- *Where'd Everybody Go?:* This game is sort of a backwards hide and seek. One person hides and everybody goes to look for him. The first to find him is "it."

- *Backwards Mother May I:* In a fun twist on the old favorite, the person who is "it" stands on the starting line and the players stand on the finish line with their back to "it." All steps are taken backwards until they get to the starting line. When the players say "May I?", the response which allows them to proceed is "Yes, you can" rather than "Yes, you may." If they move on the wrong response, they have to start over.

- *Blowin' Upstream:* Make a ramp out of heavy cardboard and lean it against a coffee table. Players blow a cotton ball "up" the ramp and the first to have his ball on the table is the winner.

- *Lucky Guess:* Have the children guess the number of pieces of candy in a jar and the one with the guess farthest from the actual number is the winner. Don't tell the children ahead of time about the twist in the game.

ENTERTAINMENT

REFRESHMENTS

Any kind of wacky food would be delightful:

Peanut butter sandwiches with peanut butter on the outside, bread on the inside
Upside-down ice cream cones
Hamburgers in hot dog buns
Hot dogs in taco shells
Pineapple upside down cake (of course!)

Silly hats
Sunglasses for shade
Vanishing ink
Crayons upside down in a box
Balloon with guests' names written backwards
A polaroid picture of everyone from behind
Magic novelties—hand buzzers, fly in an ice cube, snappy gum

FAVORS

BALLOON BLAST

Probably the most common thread among parties, aside from the giggles and the smiles, is the balloon. So why not build a whole party around these magnificent crowd pleasers!

INVITATIONS

PLACE
TIME
DATE

Write the message on an inflated balloon, then place the deflated balloon in an envelope with instructions to blow it up for a great surprise.

Place the party information on a small piece of paper, then put it inside a balloon and blow it up and tie it. Tag the balloon with instructions to pop it to see what's inside. (Of course, these would need to be hand delivered.)

Cut several different colors of circles from construction paper and arrange on paper to look like balloons. Write party info on the various balloons.

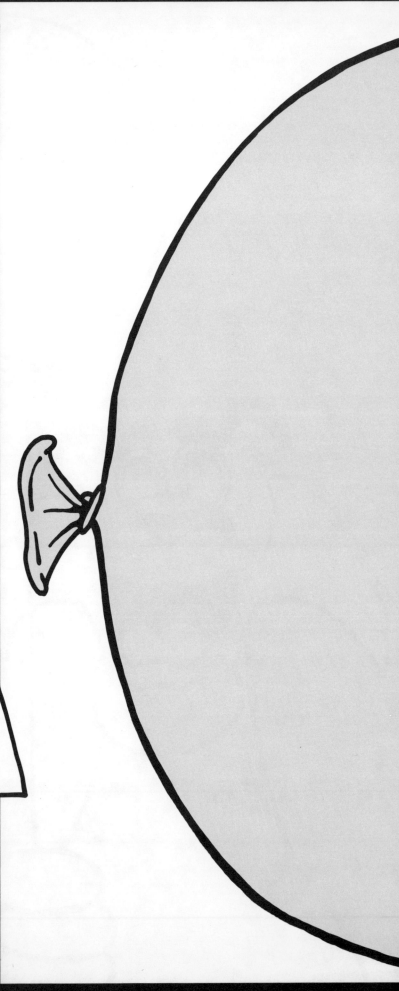

- *Hot Balloon:* The children sit in a circle and pass the inflated balloon around and across circle as though it were hot.

- *Knee Hop:* The first player on each of two relay teams hops to a designated point with an inflated balloon between his knees. If it falls out, he must put it back and start from there until he gets back to his line. The next player repeats the action until all have had a turn.

- *Musical Balloons:* Instead of having one chair missing, as in musical chairs, the last chair has an inflated balloon on the seat. When the music stops, each player must find a chair, and the last player must sit on and pop the balloon. Then play continues with a fresh balloon.

- *Balloon Jets:* All players stand on a line with untied, inflated balloons. At the signal, each lets go and watches his balloon sail through the air. The balloon that goes the farthest wins.

- *Who's Got the Hot Air?:* Give each child a balloon and allow him six puffs to see how big he can blow up his balloon. The largest wins.

- *Greetings from Cleveland:* Each child attaches a message and name and address to a helium balloon. Release the balloons and, with luck, in a few days the children will receive responses from new faraway friends.

- *Balloon Blow:* All players line up on the floor on hands and knees. The first to blow his inflated balloon across the finish line is the winner.

- *Balloon Juggle:* If you've got lots of time, give each child a balloon and see who can keep his in the air the longest. This is fun for outside. Encourage them to see how high they can hit it, have them tap it with their feet, knock it with their noses, whatever daring feats they want to try.

- *BBB (Balloon Basketball):* The first person on each of two relay teams bounces his balloon into the air, across the room, and into a "basket" (box, laundry basket). He then takes it out and returns it to the next player who repeats the action. The first team to complete the play wins.

- *Balloon Animals:* Give children a good supply of long, skinny balloons for shaping into animals and see what they come up with. Make up imaginary animals and give them names.

ENTERTAINMENT

REFRESHMENTS

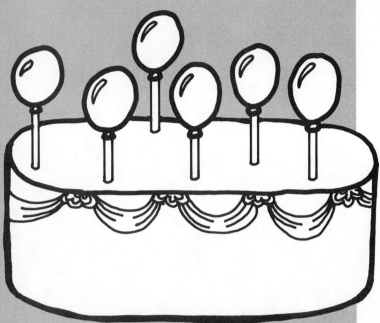

Mylar balloons
Bubbles
Bubble gum
Balloon animals
Beach balls
Small box or basket of candy
   tied under an inflated
   balloon to look like a hot
   air balloon

Balloon Cake—Decorate
a cake with tiny inflated
balloons tied onto straws
and then placed on the cake.

Cupcake Balloons—Place
a straw in the side of the
cupcake to make it look like
a balloon.

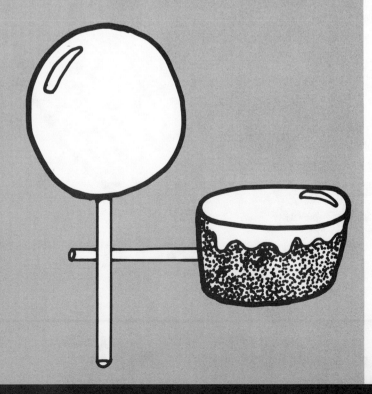

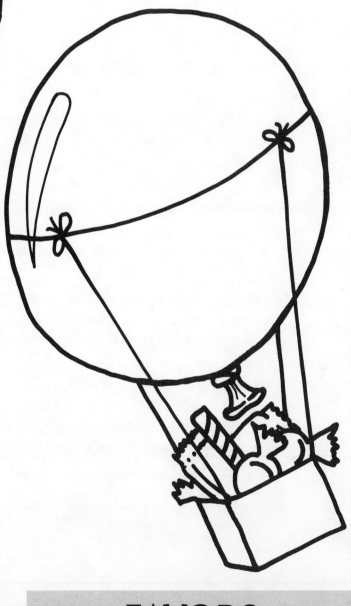

FAVORS

What better time to celebrate than the day focusing on friendship and love! Try our traditional Valentine's Day party ideas or elaborate with a fresh idea. Plan a tea party for girls where guests are invited to come dressed up in Mom's fancy clothes and shoes. Or how about a cookie decorating party where guests enjoy heart-shaped sugar cookies they have decorated themselves with icing, red hots, red sugar, or peppermint candies?

HAVE A HEART

INVITATIONS

Invitations may be as simple as a heart cut out of red paper or as fancy as a home-made valentine dressed up with stickers, lace, and doilies. Party news can be written on the face of the heart or inside a folded one.

You might also write the party information on a big red heart and then cut it into puzzle pieces and put it in an envelope. The children must then solve the puzzle in order to understand the message.

- *Make Your Own Heart:* Give everyone a red piece of paper and have them tear it into a heart shape behind their backs.

- *What's in a Name?:* Give each guest a sheet of paper and pencil and allow them five minutes to figure out how many words they can spell with the letters in the word VALENTINE.

- *Guess the Hot Dots:* Fill a jar beforehand with candy hearts or red hots and let the children take turns guessing the number of pieces of candy inside. The child guessing the closest number may take the jar home.

- *Seeing Red:* Give everyone a piece of paper and pencil and allow them five minutes to name as many red objects as they can think of in the time limit. The child with the longest list wins.

- *Broken Hearts:* Cut large red paper hearts into puzzle pieces as suggested under "Invitations" above and give each child one in an envelope or paper sack. The first child to assemble his heart wins.

- *Heart Toss:* Before the party, cut a large heart shape out of red poster board. Cut out eye, nose, and mouth shapes and mount over the open side of an empty cardboard box. The children may toss beanbags (red, heart-shaped ones would be great, but any kind would do) into the box, scoring points for putting them through the different holes. Eyes could be worth ten points, mouth twenty-five, and nose fifty, for example. The largest point holder wins. If you have made red heart-shaped beanbags, everyone could take home a prize: their own beanbag.

- *Matchmaker:* Cut paper hearts into two jagged pieces; give each child one half of a heart. Children seek out a friend who holds the matching heart half. First to find his partner wins.

  Variation: Write on each half of a heart one name of a famous pair—the male's name on one half, the female's on the other. Children seek out their other half. Be sure to choose couples that are familiar to the age group (Mork and Mindy, Mickey and Minnie, Kermit and Miss Piggy, etc.)

ENTERTAINMENT

REFRESHMENTS

A simple heart-shaped cake can be made by baking an 8-inch square layer and one round 8-inch layer. Cut the round layer in half and place each half on adjacent sides of the square, as in the diagram. Frost with pink or white icing and decorate with candies if desired.

Or try Valentine cookies, red homemade lollipops, red finger jello (see Resource Section for recipe) cut into heart shapes with a cookie cutter, or cinnamon popcorn. Red fruit punch or pink lemonade is a must at any Valentine party.

Red felt beanbags can be made easily by sewing together two heart shapes, leaving a small opening for beans, popcorn, or gravel. After stuffing, sew together the small opening. A face can be created by gluing on two round eyes and a smiling mouth, both cut from black or white felt.

Red candy and valentine stickers are tried-and-true favorites. Check your local toy and novelty store for seasonal party favors.

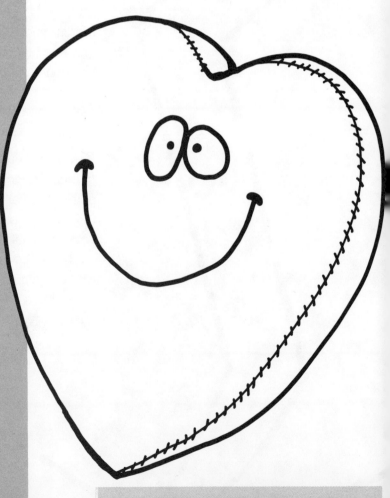

FAVORS

THE LAST BELL

There's no better way to celebrate the last day of school than to get friends together after that last bell rings. If weather cooperates, being outdoors would be terrific, either in your background or a neighborhood park.

INVITATIONS

TIME:
DATE:
PLACE:

Simply use notebook paper to extend the invitation.

Create a blackboard out of black construction paper and write the party news in white chalk. Frame the blackboard in brown paper.

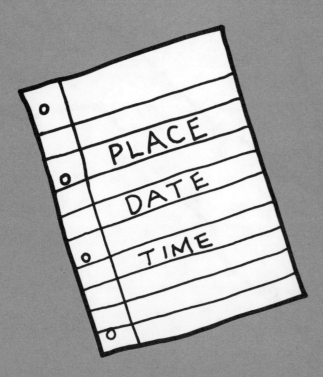

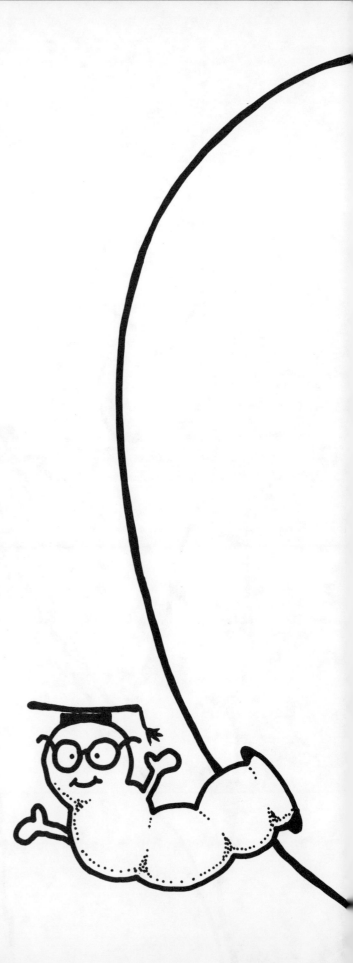

Set your party up as a day in school—with some obvious differences.

- *Readin':*

   Choose two teams for a relay race. Contestants carry a book to the end of the path, sit in a chair, open the book, read the first two lines, then run back and hand it to the next person in line. The first team to complete the course wins.

   Also as a relay race, each child walks with a book balanced on his head to a certain point and back. If the book falls off, he has to stop and put it back on before proceeding.

   A good quiet "reading" game would be to have the children unscramble school-related words, such as "tehrtaimci" (arithmetic), "lnpice" (pencil), "akcrbbdalo" (blackboard). You could do this individually with pencil and paper, with the first person completing the list winning, or you could do it one word at a time, writing on a big chart or blackboard. The first child to yell out the word gets a point.

- *'Ritin':*

   Tape a large piece of paper to the wall. Blindfold the children and have them attempt to write a message, such as "I will not talk in school." The "best" handwriting wins. The children will think it's great to see how badly they have written. You may also do this by having the children use the hand opposite the one they usually use for writing.

- *'Rithmetic:*

   Let the children guess the number of candies or gum balls in a jar. Closest to the correct number wins the jar.

- *Recess!:*

   Play an active game outside such as tag or football.

   Have a tongue twister contest. Try twisters such as "red leather, yellow leather," "toy boat," "rubber baby buggy bumpers," and repeat five times perfectly to win.

   Spit Ball Throwing Contest—Children can chew small pieces of paper to make spit balls and have a contest to see who can throw them the farthest. This may sound unpleasant, but when will they ever have the opportunity to do it again?

   Running in the Halls—The children line up for a race from one point to another. The first one "out to recess" wins.

   Let the children pantomime for each other what they plan to do during the summer. The others try to guess.

ENTERTAINMENT

REFRESHMENTS

Let the children make their own pizzas, submarines, tacos, or sundaes. See Resource Section for ideas and recipes.

Pizzas can be made by preparing dough in advance and pressing into a pizza pan or cookie sheet. Children may spread on pizza sauce and decorate their own portion with such ingredients as hamburger, pepperoni, sausage, olives, onions, cheese, etc. A simple, individual pizza may be made by using an English muffin half rather than pizza crust.

Submarine sandwiches can be "built" on individual French bread loaves. For a special touch, order a five-foot-long submarine loaf which can then be cut into smaller sections for eating. Each child might be in charge of placing one ingredient on the bread. Use salami, bologna, ham, a variety of cheeses, pickles, olives, lettuce, and tomatoes.

Sundaes are fun and easy to fix. Give each child a bowl and let them go to it! Toppings could include a variety of sauces, nuts, bananas, cherries, and whipped cream.

VEHA A
DOGO SMUMRE

School-related items such as chewing gum, apples, small slates, and chalk are fun mementos. Send the children home with homework such as putting together a puzzle or unscrambling a secret message in code. The message could read "Have A Good Summer!"

FAVORS

GO FOURTH

Celebrating our nation's birthday provides a star-spangled opportunity to establish family traditions. In our fast-changing world, children love to participate in the old-fashioned and patriotic festivities of days gone by.

INVITATIONS

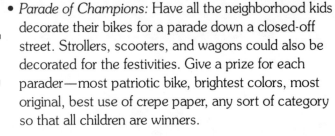

Print or type the invitation and party information on a small piece of paper and tuck it inside a small cardboard tube. Wrap the tube in red or blue crepe or tissue paper, leaving enough paper extending over edges of tube so you can pinch together and tie with yarn or ribbon to seal open ends. Hand deliver your "firecracker."

Print party information on small piece of paper. Roll it up inside a small inexpensive flag and tie with yarn. Your friends will enjoy unfurling the flag to find the message.

- *Parade of Champions:* Have all the neighborhood kids decorate their bikes for a parade down a closed-off street. Strollers, scooters, and wagons could also be decorated for the festivities. Give a prize for each parader—most patriotic bike, brightest colors, most original, best use of crepe paper, any sort of category so that all children are winners.

- *Fortune Teller:* Have someone dress up in exotic clothes with lots of jewelry and sit down with the children to read their palms. The sillier the fortunes, the better.

- *Seed Spitting Contest:* After the watermelon has been devoured, line the children up to see who can spit the seeds the farthest. A few practice rounds might be a good idea before the big spit-off.

- *Hoppy Fourth:* Line the children up in gunny sacks for an old-fashioned sack race. Nice soft grass would make the best playing field.

- *Water Shoot-Out:* Place a faraway target such as an empty can on a fence post and give each child five seconds to knock it off with the water from a hose.

- *Pelt the Parent:* Cut a hole in a sheet or large piece of cardboard and have a willing adult stick his head through. The contestants then throw rolled up socks at the target. Probably two throws will be enough—with careful instructions to be very "gentle."

- *Three-Legged Race:* With partners stand side by side, tie their inner legs together with a piece of nylon hose or belt. They then race against other pairs to the finish line.

- *Marching Musical Chairs:* Play musical chairs to "Stars and Stripes Forever." Or have the children stand on stars cut from construction paper rather than sitting on chairs.

- *Old-Fashioned Footraces:* Hop on one foot, run backwards, skip, race with book balanced on your head, crab walk, duck walk—these all sound so simple but often prove to be the most fun.

- *Water Balloon Toss:* With two lines facing each other, give opposite players water balloons. They throw to the person across from them, take a step backwards, then that player throws the balloon to them in return, steps back, and so forth, until someone misses and therefore gets wet!

Get out all the yard games—croquet, volleyball, horseshoes—and invite the whole neighborhood. Perhaps you could spread the games around several yards.

Invite everyone to bring their favorite homemade pie and have a contest to see whose is the favorite.

Have each family bring a "white elephant" and hold a raffle. It's great fun to see if what you take home can be any worse than what you donated to the cause.

ENTERTAINMENT

REFRESHMENTS

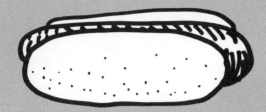

What better time for a pot-luck, picnic, or barbecue? You can't beat these all-American favorites:

Hot dogs
Hamburgers
Barbecue beef or pork
Corn on the cob
Apple pie
Homemade ice cream
Lemonade
Watermelon

Check your nearby toy or carnival supply store for patriotic or summertime novelties, like:

Small American flags
Patriotic hats
Red, white, blue balloons
Streamers for bike handles

FAVORS

You can't miss having a good time with a Halloween party because the children are so excited to be in costume that everything else is twice as much fun!

INVITATIONS

Write party information on six-inch squares of white paper. Wrap the invitation around a Tootsie Pop or other large round sucker. Tie with orange or black yarn and hand deliver.

Whooooo Wants You? Cut from colored paper the owl shape as shown at the right.

Cut from black paper a bat like the one below. Wings open to show the party news written in white or silver paint pen.

Visit a pumpkin patch and let the children pick out their own pumpkin. Head home for a pumpkin carving contest. Younger children can draw a face with black marking pen.

- *Bat, Bat, Dracula:* See Games Section for rules to "Duck, Duck, Goose," changing words to "Bat, Bat, Dracula."

- *Bat Caves:* Toss bean bags into coffee cans that have been marked with different point values.

- *Pumpkin Faces:* Mount a large jack-o'-lantern face cut from orange poster board on the open side of an empty box. The eyes, nose, and mouth have been cut out as a target through which the children throw bean bags.

- *Peanut Hunt:* Weather permitting, cover a designated section of your yard with lots of peanuts in the shell. Give each

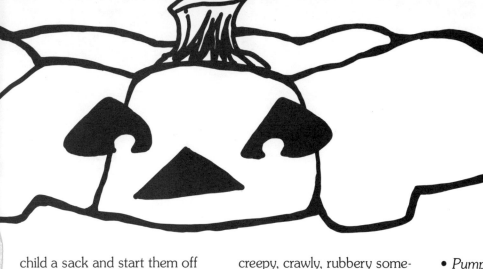

child a sack and start them off on a great hunt! It's fun to throw in plastic spiders every now and then. When you're concentrating on peanuts, spiders can catch you by surprise! The child with the most peanuts is the winner.

- *Bobbing for Apples:* A few tips to remember if you try this old classic—try to choose apples with stems for easy pick-up, especially if young children will be playing. Also, be sure to have lots of towels handy for wet faces! A scarf for the girls to use to tie back their hair would be good to have on hand.

- *Fish Pond:* This game is especially good for small children! To play you will need a fishing pole made from a broom handle or long stick with a string tied to the end and a clothespin or cup attached to the string end. Suspend a sheet in a doorway. Children toss their fishing line over the top of the suspended sheet to "fish." An adult hiding behind the sheet attaches a

creepy, crawly, rubbery something to the hook and throws it back over the sheet to the child.

- *Pin the Nose on the Pumpkin:* Sound familiar? Make an orange pumpkin face from poster board including all the features but the nose. Blindfold the first child, place a black paper triangle in his hand, twirl him around, and give him a turn at sticking the nose on the appropriate spot. Place double-stick tape on the back of the triangles so they will stick to the pumpkin. The child closest to the correct spot wins.

- *Witches Relay:* Divide the children into two relay teams. Each team is given a broom which they ride to a given point and back. The first team finished wins.

- *Doughnut on a String:* Tie doughnuts to the ends of pieces of string hung from the ceiling. The children put their hands behind their backs and at the signal begin eating the doughnuts. The first child to finish his doughnut wins.

- *Pumpkin Pond:* Another good game for small children. Get out the plastic swimming pool from summer or a large washtub and fill with water. Float small plastic pumpkins in the water. Inside these pumpkins place directions for actions for the children to do, such as "cackle like a witch," "fly like a bat," "hop around the house on one foot," etc. As each child picks a pumpkin, he acts out his task.
Variation: Put a number inside the pumpkins, each number coinciding with a small prize.

- *Corny Contest:* Guess the number of candy corn pieces in a container. The winner gets—what else?—the candy corn!

- *Costume Parade:* Have all the kids march around the yard in their costumes and be ready with your camera!

ENTERTAINMENT

REFRESHMENTS

Caramel Apples—A great variation on this is to pour melted caramels over a bowl of apple slices. It's not as messy and the children tend to eat more of the apple. (See Resource Section.)

Popcorn Balls—Easy recipe in Resource Section.

Witches' Brew—Float pieces of dry ice in orange drink. (Dry ice can be purchased from an ice house.) Add more spooky fun by floating plastic spiders in the brew, making sure each child gets one in his cup. (In glass container, be sure to put dry ice in container after liquid is poured!)

Ghost Cake—Bake your favorite sheet cake and cut it into the shape of a ghost. Frost with fluffy white frosting. Cider and doughnuts are Halloween favorites!

Pumpkin Cookies—Frost your favorite sugar cookie or peanut butter cookie with orange frosting. Make a face on the cookie to look like a jack-o'-lantern by using chocolate chips for the features.

Plan a ghoulish menu and put it on the invitation, with the explanation, of course! Here are some suggestions:

Snake eyes (peas or olives)
Skeleton parts (shoestring
   potatoes)
Vampire patties (hamburgers)
Witches' brew (steaming
   punch)

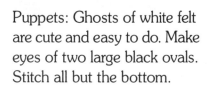

Puppets: Ghosts of white felt are cute and easy to do. Make eyes of two large black ovals. Stitch all but the bottom.

Spiders: Paint a 3- or 4-inch styrofoam ball with black spray paint. Stick eight black pipe cleaners into the ball at appropriate spots for legs. Wiggly eyes can be added also.

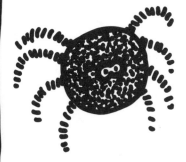

Arm Bands: Cut a strip of black felt about two inches wide and about two inches longer than the circumference of the child's upper arm. Sew velcro at the ends of the band so that it will stay around the arm. Cut the letters "BOO" out of orange felt or reflective mylar and glue onto the arm band.

Ghost Lollipops: Place white tissue paper over a Tootsie Pop with a rubber band or black and orange yarn. Draw eyes and mouth with black marker.

Spiders on a Leash: Use a large black ball from ball fringe, glue black pipe cleaners on the ball for legs,

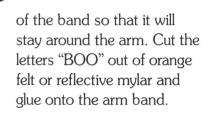

and then dangle from a 24-inch dowel stick with fish line. You may also add tiny wiggly eyes and a red paper dot on the stomach.

Trick or Treat Bags: Purchase a Halloween print or plain black or orange fabric. Cut a simple rectangle shape, sew sides and bottom, make a casing at the top, and pull through a piece of black ribbon and tie.

Bean Bags: These are terrific in pumpkin shapes or as bats.

Other ideas: Shop at your local novelty supply store for creepy critters like rubber bats, spiders and insects, plastic pumpkins, and Halloween pencils. Cyalume light sticks are generally available at variety stores for under $1.

FAVORS

INVITATIONS

All ages enjoy getting together at this festive time of year.

Stuff the invitation inside a simple felt stocking.

Cut a tree from construction paper, writing your message on the ornaments.

Gift wrap your invitation inside a small box.

PLACE

TIME

DATE

- *Candy Cane Hunt:* Before guests arrive, hide small, wrapped candy canes around the room for children to hunt. Child who finds the most wins.

- *Chain Gang:* Give each child red and green paper strips and tape or a stapler. Race to see who can make the longest paper chain in a given period of time.

- *Trim the Tree:* The children form two relay teams with each member given a small wrapped candy cane. At the signal, the first person in each line runs to the Christmas tree, unwraps his candy cane, places it on the tree, and runs back to touch the next person in line. The first team to have placed all their candy canes on the tree wins.

- *Pin the Star on the Christmas Tree* or *Pin the Nose on Rudolph:* A variation on the old standby, Pin the Tail on the Donkey.

- *Calendar Toss:* Draw a large calendar of the month of December on poster board and place it on the floor. The children then line up and take turns trying to throw a jingle bell so that it will land on December 25th. The person coming the closest wins.

- *Guess the Gift:* Wrap up different presents in all shapes and sizes of boxes. Have the children guess what might be inside by shaking the packages.

- *Make Ornaments:* Children can create Christmas ornaments by molding salt dough into Christmas shapes. (See the Resource Section for salt dough recipe.) Dough can also be rolled out and cut with cookie cutters into Christmas designs. Also try cutting Christmas shapes from felt into such shapes as trees, wreaths, and candy canes. Children can glue on decorations such as glitter, sequins, and rick-rack trim.

- *O Christmas Tree:* Let each child guess how many ornaments are on your tree. Winner might take home a small ornament for his own tree.

ENTERTAINMENT

- *Gingerbread House Decorating:* Invite three or four families over for an evening of gingerbread house decorating. It is a good idea to have the houses pre-assembled so that all the guests need to do is decorate. Use the gingerbread dough recipe in the Resource Section or the simpler graham cracker/milk carton design also listed. Punch and cookies would be a nice touch for a fun evening. If gingerbread houses seem to be too ambitious an undertaking, have the families decorate large gingerbread boys and girls with frosting and candies.

- *Cookie Exchange:* This is a super way to enjoy sampling all your friends' favorite Christmas cookies. Invite the children to bring a batch of their favorite homemade cookies along with a basket or box for taking cookies home. After all cookies are placed on the table, the children walk around the table with baskets taking two cookies from each batch until the cookies are gone. Refreshments could include the hostess' own cookies or samples from the table.

- *Caroling Party:* Nothing brings out the Christmas spirit more than familiar Christmas carols. They are a wonderful common denominator. Whether families or friends, everyone will get caught up in this cheery holiday tradition.

  As the carolers arrive, have them decorate the cover of pre-assembled songbooks with glitter, felt, markers, old Christmas cards, etc. These make great keepsakes.

  A beautiful alternative to neighborhood caroling might include a visit to a hospital, nursing home, or the homes of shut-ins with small child-made gifts, ornaments, homemade cookies, or additional songbooks.

  When the songfest has ended, return home to a warm, glowing fire and hot wassail, egg nog, doughnuts, or holiday cookies.

Other Christmas party ideas include:

Ornament making
Cookie decorating
Tree trimming

ENTERTAINMENT

REFRESHMENTS

Christmas cookies
Red or green punch
Candy canes
Red or green popcorn balls

Crispy Rice Snowmen: Using the recipe found in the Resource Section, shape the mixture into two or three balls and stack. Use raisins or chocolate chips for features.

Christmas Trees: Place a sugar cone upside down on a small paper plate. Frost the cone with green frosting and then let the children decorate with red hots, chocolate candies, or other brightly colored candy.

Give ornaments made from salt dough (see Resource Section) or felt candy cane covers.

To make a horse head cover, draw around the curved end of your candy cane onto a paper pattern, adding ¼ inch to all edges. Add the shape of a horse's nose and ears and cut out. Sew very close to all edges, except for bottom of neck. Enclose cloth fringe in a bright color along neck edge before sewing. Glue on wiggly eyes.

Favors might also include:

Molded chocolate lollipops: Check the yellow pages in the telephone book under "Candy and Confectionery" to locate sucker molds.

Decorated gingerbread men.

Gift exchange: Have each child bring an inexpensive gift, assign a number to each and then have the children draw numbers, making sure no one gets his own gift. You could have each child bring a small gift to be given to a needy family or Toys for Tots as admittance to the party.

FAVORS

WINTER PICNIC

Mid-winter can be a challenge for entertaining children since sending them outside to play is often difficult in the cold weather. On the worst days, an indoor winter picnic can solve this problem. Find a good-sized room and scoot back the furniture. Have the children wear shorts under their jeans so they can pretend that the sun is shining and the temperature is warm.

PLACE
TIME
DATE

Use a brown lunch bag as an envelope and write the pertinent party information on a napkin to tuck inside.

A big sun with the party news written across it would be a welcome harbinger of spring.

PLACE
TIME
DATE

INVITATIONS

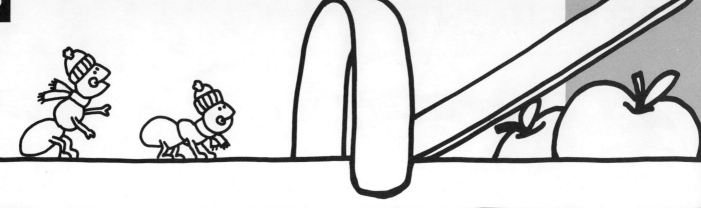

- *Memory Game:* The first child says "I'm going on a picnic and I'm going to take an *ant*." The next child repeats what the first child has said and adds something that begins with "B," the next child "C," and so forth. When a child is unable to remember what has been said, he is out.

- *Indoor Tag:* Have the children play tag on their knees.

- *Peanut Golf:* Have a course laid out using cups as holes. The children use a pencil and a peanut as the club and ball.

- *Bubble Gum Blowing Contest:* This is probably more appropriate for children seven and older. Prizes for biggest bubble, longest lasting bubble, oddest shaped bubble, and smallest bubble can be awarded.

- *Whistling Contest:* Form two relay teams. First child in each line eats a cracker, runs to a certain point, whistles, then runs back to touch the next teammate who repeats task. The first team to complete wins.

- *Balloon Blow:* Each relay team receives an inflated balloon. The first players push the balloon with their noses to an end point, pick up the balloon, and return it to the next teammate. The first team finished wins.

Another good entertainment idea would be to have different games set up all over the room (video games, ping pong, gin rummy, and Monopoly, for example) and have a schedule of who plays each at what time. When it is time to switch, each child takes over the person's place where he has been assigned, using the position or score of that player. Play then continues. You might want to do this with several different board games of three or four players each.

ENTERTAINMENT

REFRESHMENTS

Put a red-checked tablecloth on the floor or serve food in baskets lined with bandanas. Sandwiches, chips, cupcakes, fruit, or fried chicken would be fun. Also, you could cook hot dogs at the fireplace and roast marshmallows for dessert. Or make "s'mores," tucking a roasted marshmallow along with half of a milk chocolate bar between two graham crackers.

Good picnic mementos might include:

Squirt guns
Inexpensive sunglasses
Bubbles and bubble pipes
Brown bags with each child's name printed on them (print them yourself or purchase them at a specialty shop)

FAVORS

MORE WAYS TO CELEBRATE

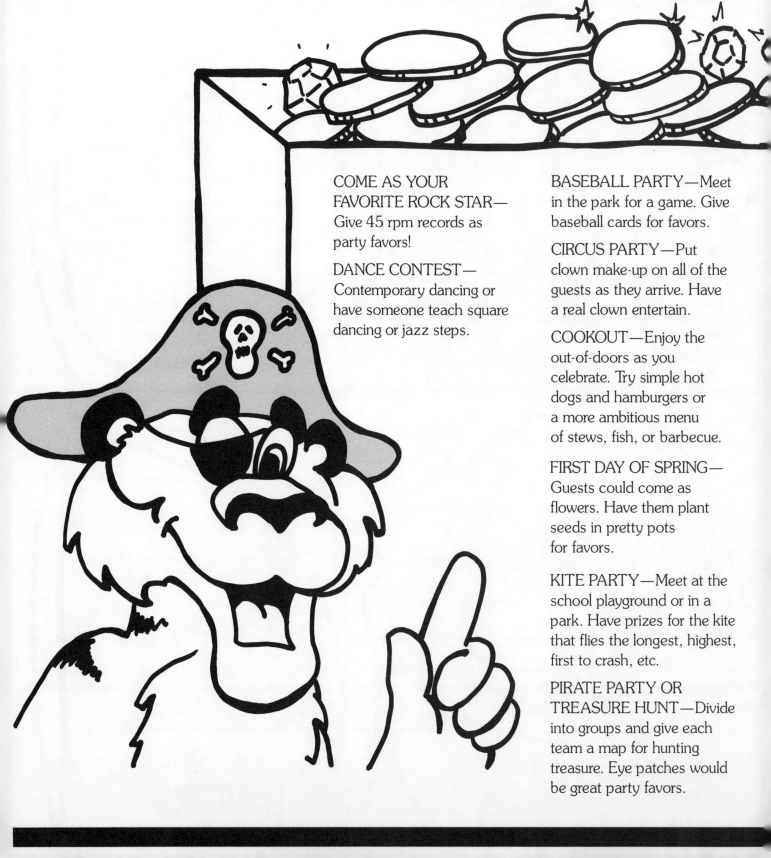

COME AS YOUR FAVORITE ROCK STAR—Give 45 rpm records as party favors!

DANCE CONTEST—Contemporary dancing or have someone teach square dancing or jazz steps.

BASEBALL PARTY—Meet in the park for a game. Give baseball cards for favors.

CIRCUS PARTY—Put clown make-up on all of the guests as they arrive. Have a real clown entertain.

COOKOUT—Enjoy the out-of-doors as you celebrate. Try simple hot dogs and hamburgers or a more ambitious menu of stews, fish, or barbecue.

FIRST DAY OF SPRING—Guests could come as flowers. Have them plant seeds in pretty pots for favors.

KITE PARTY—Meet at the school playground or in a park. Have prizes for the kite that flies the longest, highest, first to crash, etc.

PIRATE PARTY OR TREASURE HUNT—Divide into groups and give each team a map for hunting treasure. Eye patches would be great party favors.

SNOW PARTY—Have everyone over for hot chocolate and doughnuts, then go outside to build snowmen, forts, or have a well-organized snowball fight.

SPACE PARTY—Visit a nearby space exhibit at a museum. Have children make space helmets from discarded, clean ice cream tubs.

TEA PARTY—Great chance to dress up! Invite parents or a favorite teacher.

HOBO PARTY—Great costume possibilities!

TWENTIES PARTY—Teach everyone to do the Charleston.

SLEDDING PARTY—Find a park with a big hill. Warm up afterwards with cocoa.

COME-AS-YOU-ARE PARTY—Call the guests a few days in advance at an odd hour to invite them to the party. They must dress exactly as they are at the time of the call!

SURPRISE BREAKFAST—Either surprise guests by waking them up and dragging them out of bed, or surprise the honoree by getting him or her out of bed.

GAME SHOW—Do a take-off on a popular TV game show by revising it a bit for home use. Have the guests guess the cost of certain items, give them a choice of three boxes from which to choose prizes, then try to bargain with them to take an alternate prize (bubble gum, frisbee, etc.) instead. Some of the prizes in the boxes could be desirable, some should be outrageous.

CARTOON PARTY—Have guests come as their favorite cartoon character. Show cartoons for entertainment.

ZOO PARTY—Visit the zoo. Dress up as animals. Make animal masks.

DRESS-UP PARTY—Serve a nice sit-down dinner. Could be fun for a change!

COME-AS-YOUR-MOTHER/FATHER—Good excuse for dressing up in Mom's or Dad's clothes.

FOOTBALL PARTY—Set up an easy game of tag football on a pretty day.

SOCCER PARTY—Can be played inside or out.

BIKE RODEO—Have guests decorate their bikes and then have races (obstacle courses, gliding without peddling, etc.).

NERD PARTY—Guests dress up as real nerds. Plan some sort of activity where they will be outside where others will see them (scavenger hunt, outside games, etc.)

STUFF A SCARECROW—Great for Halloween season! Have guests bring clothes for a scarecrow, then you provide the straw and poles.

A few general rules need to be followed so that your games will be successful.

First, be sure your explanation is simple yet understandable. A practice round is a good idea to make sure everyone is ready. Younger children especially need to feel comfortable with what they are doing, or they might choose not to participate. Make sure the game moves quickly and everyone plays by the rules. Do not be afraid to stop a game if it is getting out of hand or the children are losing interest. Also, in games such as "Duck, Duck, Goose" or "Drop the Handkerchief," see that everyone gets a turn. Individual prizes are discouraged at parties but team prizes to the winners and consolation prizes (lollipops, bubble gum, etc.) leave everyone with a good, happy feeling. Have all of the game "props" ready ahead of time so that you do not lose your audience as you prepare.

Guess Who I Am? (Age 4 and up)

One player goes to the front of the group and hides his eyes against the wall with his back to the group. The hostess points to one person in the group who goes to the front, stands behind the player, and says "Guess who I am?" in a silly or disguised voice. The player gets two guesses to identify the voice, and then the voice becomes the guesser.

What Time Is It? (Age 7 and up)

The children sit in a circle and when the hostess says "Go," each starts counting silently to themselves, trying to guess when sixty seconds has gone by. When they think it's time, they raise their hand. Meanwhile, using a clock with a second hand or a stopwatch, the hostess times a minute. The child raising his hand closest to the exact sixty seconds is the winner.

Potato Push (Preschool and up)

Potatoes are great game tools and can be used in a number of ways. Have the children roll them across the ground with their noses or feet. They can hop with a potato between their knees or thighs. Or they may put potatoes in a spoon and carry them to the finish line, either in their hand or their teeth.

Fish (Preschool through 8)

Place small gifts, wrapped and tied with bows, in an empty plastic pool or large box. The children then pass around a fishing pole (broom handle with string and bent paper clip at the end) and try to snare the present of their choice, hooking the bow with the paper clip. This is a good activity for distributing favors at the end of the party.

Flag Tag (Age 6 and up)

Each player puts a handkerchief or piece of cloth in a back pocket or waistband. Part of the "flag" should be hanging out. The players then run around trying to grab everyone's handkerchief without losing their own. Anyone who has lost his sits on the sidelines. The last person to survive with their flag is the winner. No tripping and no tackling rules must be strictly enforced.

Huckle Buckle Beanstalk (Age 4 and up)

Choose a small object to hide. Start the game by having the children cover their eyes while you put the object in a spot that is visible but not too easily seen. The children search the room with their hands behind their backs, trying to spot the object. As soon as they see it they look away and say "Huckle Buckle Beanstalk." The game continues until everyone has seen the object. The first to have seen the object is "it" and re-hides the object.

Poor Kitty (Preschool and up)

One child is chosen to be the "kitty." The rest of the group sits on the floor in a circle. The kitty crawls on the floor and sadly stops at each child to say "meow." That child must pat the kitty without the trace of a smile. The kitty then crawls to the next person and continues doing so until someone finally smiles or giggles. That person becomes the next kitty.

Duck, Duck, Goose (Preschool and up)

The players sit in a circle on the floor. The person who is "it" walks around the outside of the circle, touching the players on the head as he passes by and saying "duck" as he taps each. Eventually, "it" must touch someone and say "goose." Goose jumps up and chases "it" back to his place in the circle, trying to get there first. If "it" makes it back without being tagged, then "goose" becomes "it" and play resumes. If "it" is tagged, then he is "it" again.

Musical Papers (Preschool and up)

This game is like musical chairs except the children stand on a piece of paper instead of sitting on chairs. Papers are arranged in a circle with one less piece than the number of children participating. The children walk around the circle as the music plays. When the music stops, they must find a paper and stand on it. One person will be extra and so is eliminated. A piece of paper is removed and play resumes until two children are left with one spot. The final play-off is exciting! The papers can be cut into appropriate shapes for your particular party (pumpkins for Halloween, trees for Christmas, hearts for Valentine's Day, etc.).

Truth or Consequences (Age 8 and up)

Make a list of ten silly true or false questions and a list of ten silly consequences. For a wrong answer, the child must do the consequence of the corresponding number. For example, *Question:* Abraham Lincoln was the first president of the United States. True or false? *Consequence:* Pretend you are fishing in the ocean and have just landed a shark! Naturally, the children may try to answer incorrectly in order to pay the "consequence."

Line Tag (Kindergarten and up)

The person who is "it" chases the others until he catches one and tags him. These two players then hold hands and run together to catch another player to tag them. That person then joins the group, joining the hand-holding line, continuing until all are caught. When the line reaches four to six players, the group splits to form two groups.

Guess the Gift (Preschool and up)

Before each gift is opened, the giver can offer up to three clues as to what's inside while the partygoers guess. Then the gift is opened.

Shall We Dance? (Kindergarten through second grade)

You need an odd number to play this game. Children start by dancing with a partner while the extra person dances with a broomstick. When the music stops, everyone changes partners and the extra person dances with the broom.

Interviews (Kindergarten and up)

Divide the children into pairs. The person in charge asks questions of one person, but the other answers for him. For example, the leader might say "What is your favorite food?" to one child while his partner answers for him. There is no winner in this game but it is an entertaining activity.

Burst Your Bubble (Age 6 and up)

Place activities, fortunes, or silly directions inside a balloon and blow it up. Each child selects a balloon, pops it, and then performs as instructed or reads his fortune aloud to the delight of the others. Some suggestions for the activities might be to sing "Jingle Bells" while hopping on one foot, name at least six blue things in the room, pronounce all the kids' names backwards, etc.

Chatter Bee (Age 5 and up)

The players line up in two rows, back to back. The person behind you is your partner. At the signal, two players turn to face each other and both begin to talk quickly, non-stop, about anything they wish, for thirty seconds. This may be done two at a time or by the whole group at once. A judge can decide which team did the "best" talking.

Post Card Identification (Older children)

Gather twelve postcards depicting different local or famous national landmarks (Washington Monument, White House, etc.). Number the postcards 1 through 12 and display for all to see. Children are to write down the correct name of the landmark on their paper, matching the corresponding number with the landmark.

Letter Scramble (Age 9 and up)

Each child writes his first or last name on a piece of paper. Then the papers are collected and passed out at random. The children must try to make as many words as possible from the name they have received. For example, from the name "Anderson," you might find the words "read," "nose," "ran," "son," "sand," etc. A ten-minute time limit is a good idea. The child who finds the most words is the winner.

Mutt and Jeff (Age 4 and up)

The group stands in a circle with "Mutt" and "Jeff" inside. Mutt is blindfolded. He calls out his name and Jeff answers with his while Mutt tries to tag him, following his voice. As soon as Jeff is caught, he becomes the blindfolded player and Mutt picks a new Jeff. You may substitute more seasonal names for "Mutt" and "Jeff," such as "Prancer" and "Vixen," etc.

Instruction Mix-Up (Age 5 and up)

All players gather around a sheet or blanket, with each one holding onto a part of it. When the leader yells "Let go," everyone holds on; when the leader yells

"Hold on," everyone lets go. When you miss, you are out of the game and the last player remaining is the winner. The fun is in the confusion which results.

Egg Toss (Age 8 and up)

This game is much like a water balloon toss game. The group is divided into two teams. Members of each team stand facing each other and begin throwing a raw egg back and forth, taking a step back after each successful catch. The team that continues to catch the egg from the furthest distance wins.

String Maze (Age 6 and up)

Tie a prize at the end of a colored ball of string and hide the prize under a cushion, in a drawer, etc. Unwind the rest of the string, going around chair legs, behind doors, over furniture, criss-crossing as you go. Tie a pencil to the end so the child may wrap up the string as he follows the maze. Give each player a different colored string and have the different strings lap over each other to add to the challenge and the fun.

Jack Be Nimble (Age 4–7)

One child, "Jack," stands in the center of the circle of players. The group says the nursery rhyme, "Jack be nimble, Jack be quick, Jack jump over the candle-stick." When they say "Jack jump over the candlestick," Jack runs between two players in the circle. They then run in opposite directions from each other around the outside of the circle. The first one back to his original position gets to be Jack.

Twenty Questions (Age 4 and up)

One child leaves the room and everyone decides on one object in the room. When the missing child returns, he tries to guess what the object is by asking twenty questions—children may answer only "yes" or "no." When twenty questions are up or the object is guessed, another child leaves the room and a different object is chosen.

Mother May I (Age 5 and up)

All the children stand in a line, shoulder to shoulder, facing the person who is designated as "Mother." One at a time, she gives the children a direction to follow (take six baby steps, hop four steps forward, etc.). The child must first say "Mother may I?" before completing the task. If he fails to ask, he must go back to the starting point. The object is to get across the finish line first.

Stuff the Pillow Relay (Age 10 and up)

Divide the group into two or more equal teams. The first person on each team gets a pillowcase and a pillow is put at each goal line. At the signal, the first player runs up to the pillow, puts it in the pillowcase, and carries it back to the second person. That person removes the pillow, carries it back to the goal line, and gives the case to the third person, who repeats the actions of the first player and so on until everyone has participated. This game is more suitable for older children.

Memory Game (Age 8 and up)

This is a wonderful quiet game. Each child is provided with a pencil and a piece of paper. The hostess then sets before the children a tray filled with items that

can either be miscellaneous or tied in with the party theme. The children have two minutes to study the items on the tray before it is removed or covered with a towel. The children then have five minutes to write all the items they remember seeing. The child with the most items listed correctly wins.

String Hunt (Preschool and up)

Hide sixty to eighty pieces of string cut various lengths from two inches to two feet. At the signal, the children begin looking for the strings. When all or most have been found, have each child lay out his strings end to end to see who found the longest length. This is a great game for playing outside.

Card Hunt (Preschool and up)

Hide playing cards (no jokers) around the room for the children to find. One deck for every six children is a good number. Allow time for players to find the cards and then add up their points. The number cards receive face value; jacks twelve points, queens fourteen points, kings sixteen points, and aces twenty points. The child with the highest point total wins.

Ribbon Relay (especially for girls) (Ages 8 and up)

Have two teams lined up single file. The first person in each line has a ribbon tied in a bow in her hair or is wearing an article of clothing to be passed on (sweater with buttons, jacket with a zipper, etc.). At the signal, the first person unties the ribbon and ties it in a bow on the head of the next girl, etc., until the ribbon has made it all the way down the line. If an article of clothing is used, the first girl removes it, passes it on to the next girl who puts it on, takes it off, etc.

Funny Grams (Age 8 and up)

Players get a pencil and a piece of paper. The leader reads four or five letters of the alphabet and each child must think of a message that explains that code. For example, if the letters were B E Y C F, the message might be "Brian eats yellow caterpillar feet." When everyone has written their message, they are read aloud.

String Along (Age 5 and up)

Each player is given a two- to three-foot-long piece of string and a bowl of uncooked macaroni. At the signal, each begins stringing macaroni on their string and continues for three to five minutes. At the end of the time limit, the child with the longest macaroni chain wins.

Special Spot Tag (Age 4 and up)

The person who is "it" attempts to tag another. When he does, the new "it" must keep his hand on the spot on his body where he was tagged while he chases someone else to be "it." For example, if he were tagged on the shoulder, he must hold his hand there until he has tagged a new person.

Hang Out the Clothes Relay (Age 5 and up)

Divide the group into equal teams of four or more children. Each team receives five clothespins and stands in line about twenty feet from a clothesline. Each team uses the section of line that is directly across from their position. At the signal, the first person runs up and puts all five pins on the line, the next person runs up and removes them, the third person replaces them, etc.

Time's Up (Age 7 and up)

The leader hides an alarm clock or timer in the room with the alarm set for five minutes. Everyone searches for it, and as each thinks he knows where it is, he tells the leader. If he is correct, he sits down while the others continue to look. If the alarm goes off before all players find it, those still looking are out of the game and play is repeated with the remaining children.

Follow the Leader (Age 3–5)

Don't forget this old classic loved by all ages. Either a child (perhaps the birthday person) or an adult can lead. Just do whatever safe activity comes into your head—hop on one foot, flap your arms, run backwards, etc. The others do what the leader does.

Pass the Bean (Age 9 and up)

Each child receives ten beans at the beginning of the game. Everyone begins shaking hands with the other players and to every tenth person with whom you shake hands, you give a bean. The object is to try to get rid of your beans first. This is difficult because everyone else is trying to pass theirs to you at the same time.

Copy Cat (Age 4 and up)

Everyone sits in a circle on the floor. The person who is "it" covers his eyes while a leader is chosen. The leader then begins doing movements such as patting the floor, clapping his hands, rubbing his stomach, etc., while the rest of the group follows quickly. The person who is "it" tries to guess who the leader is by watching the group's movements.

Mystery Shadow (Age 4 and up)

Tie a sheet in a doorway with a light behind it. One guest at a time goes behind the sheet and does actions while the others try to guess what he is doing.

Price is Right (Age 8 and up)

Divide the group into two teams. The first player on each team tries to decide how much a particular item (can of peaches, tube of toothpaste, etc.) costs, and the person coming the closest without going over the price wins a point for his team.

Who's Got the Ring? (Age 4 and up)

The group except the person who is "it" sits in a circle and everyone places their hands on a large piece of string which is tied in a loop equivalent to the circle size. A washer, button, or ring is placed on the string and the children pass it around the circle, under their hands, while "it" tries to guess where the ring is.

Orange Relay (Age 6 and up)

The children are divided into two relay teams and the first child in each line is given an orange to tuck under his chin. At the signal, these first players turn to the person behind them in line, hands behind their backs, and try to pass the orange to that person who also must hold it tucked under his chin. This game is not only comical to play but also to watch, and as the giggles come, the oranges often drop. As this happens, the child picks up the orange, places it back under his chin, and play resumes.

Suitcase Relay (Age 8 and up)

The children are divided into two relay teams. Each team is furnished with a suitcase full of clothing such as a large dress, hat, and lady's shoes or large men's pants, sweatshirt, belt, tie, etc. At the signal, the first child in each line runs up to a designated point, carrying the suitcase. He stops, puts on the clothes in the suitcase, and runs back to his line, suitcase in hand. There he removes the clothes, places them back in the suitcase, and passes it on to the next player who repeats his actions. The clothes can be adapted to your party's theme by using cowboy clothes, sport clothes, costumes, etc.

Charades (Age 8 and up)

Divide the group into two teams. First, each team composes a list of song, book, or movie titles and writes them individually on pieces of paper. One at a time, team members draw a title from the opposing group's pile and proceed to act it out, without speaking, for their own team. Each turn is timed and the time recorded. The team that has guessed the titles in the shortest amount of time by the end of the game wins. To save time you may make up the list ahead of time. This is a great game for older children and super for adults!

Bean Bag Games (Any age)

Bean bags make a wonderful game as well as party favors. Felt bean bags are the most easily constructed, as you simply sew around the two shapes, leaving a small opening, fill with beans, rice, or popcorn, and sew up the remaining edge. The target can be made from a large box on which has been drawn some clever, appropriate figure with openings cut for the bean bags. For example: dog target, use "bone" bean bags of white felt; Cookie Monster target, use "chocolate chip cookie" bean bags; bunny target, use "Easter egg" bean bags; jack-o'-lantern target, use "bat" or "pumpkin" bean bags.

Balloon Games (All ages)

Divide the group into two teams with the children on each team paired with a partner. Standing side by side, the children lock arms. Each pair is given a blown-up balloon. At the signal, the first couple on each team bats their balloon to the goal line and back using their outside arms since their inside arms are linked. If the balloon hits the ground, they pick it up and continue batting it back to the next couple in line.

There are many fun variations for moving inflated balloons from one point to another:

1. Push balloons with noses across the finish line.
2. Hop with inflated balloons between the knees.
3. Blow balloons across the finish line.
4. Run with the balloon to the finish line and then pop it by sitting on it. (Caution: Many children won't enjoy popping balloons.)
5. Kick the balloon across the finish line.

Place a small prize or candy inside the balloon which the child retrieves when the balloon is popped, or place directions for an activity which the child may complete (sing "London Bridge," count to 100 by 3's, etc.).

Another game using balloons is to tie inflated balloons to each ankle of each player. At the signal, all players move around the room trying to pop one another's balloons by stepping on them. This can get rather heated so it is more suited to older children, but they love it. The last child to survive with at least one balloon is the winner.

Polaroid Scavenger Hunt (Age 12 and up)

This is a great twist on the old scavenger hunts where the children sometimes need to return the items they have gathered. The teams are provided with a Polaroid camera and a list of situations which they are to photograph. Use your imagination in creating this list; make some items more difficult than others. For example, finding a dead tree might be difficult but is possible. Or have the teams look for a family of five—mom, dad, two sisters, and one brother. The list should contain more situations than the teams have film for so that they won't be able to photograph everything on the list. Point values are assigned to each item and the team with the largest number of points wins. The game is terrific for older children and will come off without a hitch if certain guidelines are established. Naturally, the children must be courteous to the people they are asking to photograph, they must stay on their assigned street, and they should return to the starting point or party site when the time limit is up.

SWEET TREATS

Honey Bears

Good treat for kids to mix themselves!

Stir together 1 cup peanut butter and 2 to 3 tablespoons honey. Add powdered milk a little at a time, mixing with a wooden spoon until mixture has a dough-like consistency. Children can mold it, just like Playdough, into whatever shapes come to mind. Decorate with sprinkles, raisins, nuts, or chocolate chips.

Cut-up Cookies

A good basic recipe for sugar cookies. The dough is easy to work with.

2 cups flour
1 cup sugar
1/2 t. salt
1/2 t. baking soda
3/4 cup shortening
1 egg, beaten
1 1/2 t. vanilla

Sift dry ingredients together. Mix in shortening with two knives or pastry blender until well blended. Add egg and vanilla, and mix. Roll out and cut with cutters of desired shape. Sprinkle with sugar or sprinkles. Bake at 375 degrees for 10-12 minutes.

Crispy Treats

Cookies can be molded into any shape while warm, or can be spread into a pan and cut when cool.

1/4 cup butter
1 (10-oz.) package marshmallows
5 cups crispy rice cereal

Melt butter and marshmallows together over low heat, stirring constantly. Add crispy rice and mix well. Press into pan or desired shapes while warm with buttered fingers. Can be decorated with colored candies.

Variation: Crispy Treat squares can be made into super party treats by poking sucker or popsicle sticks into one end while warm.

Easy Popcorn Balls

Using preceding recipe for Crispy Treats, melt butter and marshmallows together, and substitute 5-6 cups popped corn for crispy rice. Mold into balls while warm. (Food coloring or 2 tablespoons flavored gelatin mix can be stirred into butter-marshmallow mixture before adding popcorn.)

Candy Ornaments

Place any hard candies on a baking sheet. (Those with flowers in the center "bloom" as they expand!) Bake at 300 degrees for 10 minutes. Let cool for several minutes, then make hole near edge with toothpick. Place fishing line through hole to hang ornament.

Big Fat Cookies

1 package cake mix
1/2 cup water
2 eggs
1 cup chocolate chips or M&M's

Prepare cake mix as directed on package, using 1/2 cup water and 2 eggs.

Leave out salad oil. Drop onto greased cookie sheet 3 inches apart. Sprinkle with candies. Bake at 375 degrees for 8-10 minutes.

Fudge Sauce for Sundaes

3/4 cup sugar
1/4 cup butter
2 squares or envelopes semi-sweet chocolate
2 T. corn syrup (white)
dash salt
1/4 cup milk
2 t. vanilla

Combine sugar, butter, chocolate, corn syrup, and salt, and cook over medium heat, stirring well. Add milk and bring to boil until thickened. Remove from heat and stir in vanilla.

Clown Cones

Easy to make—fun to eat!

Several hours before party, scoop ice cream of desired flavor onto cookie sheet covered with waxed paper. Refreeze until solid. Before serving, place sugar cone upside-down on scoop for a hat and create
a face with candies.

Lollipops

2 cups sugar
2/3 cup corn syrup (white)
1 cup hot water
food coloring
flavoring(s)

Cook sugar, syrup, and water to extreme hard crack stage (310 degrees). Stir only until sugar is dissolved. Remove any crystals that form on sides of pan. Cook slowly toward end of process in order that syrup may not scorch. Remove from heat, add coloring and flavoring, stirring only enough to mix. Drop mixture from tip of a tablespoon onto a smooth, oiled surface (such as a buttered cookie sheet), taking care to keep drops small so that they don't spread into each other. Place a tongue depressor into edge of each before it hardens, and cover with another drop of the mixture. Candies should be loosened from surface before they are completely cooled to prevent cracking.

Ice Cream Cake

A variation on the traditional party cake.

Soften your favorite flavor of ice cream and pat into a mold of your choice. (You can use a bowl, jello mold, or cake pan.) Freeze until solid. Unmold by dipping container quickly into warm water. Refreeze. Cover with whipping cream and decorate as desired.

Flower Pot Treats

Place a chocolate sandwich cookie in bottom of clean 3-inch clay pot. Fill almost to top with your favorite flavor of ice cream. Place 8–10 chocolate sandwich cookies in blender and mix until they become fine crumbs. Put these crumbs over ice cream in pots to resemble soil. Keep frozen until time to serve. Place plastic straw cut the height of pot into center and insert plastic or fresh flower into straw before serving.

Conecakes

Mix your favorite cake recipe and pour into flat-bottomed ice cream cones 2/3 full. Set the cones in a cake pan and bake at 350 degrees for 15–18 minutes. When cool, ice and decorate as desired.

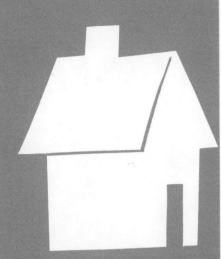

Cookies-on-a-Stick

1 cup butter or margarine
1 cup peanut butter
2 cups brown sugar (firmly packed)
2 eggs
2 1/2 cups all-purpose flour (unsifted)

1 1/2 t. baking soda
1 t. baking powder

Beat butter or margarine and peanut butter with brown sugar until creamy. Beat in eggs. Add flour, baking soda, and baking powder; mix until well blended. Shape into balls, each containing approximately 1/2 cup dough. Flatten slightly. Insert popsicle stick into cookie about halfway, making sure stick does not show through dough. Place 3 inches apart on greased cookie sheet. Bake in 350 degree oven 12-15 minutes or until slightly golden. Cookies can be decorated with faces or names.

Gingerbread Houses

This recipe is enough to make a gingerbread house and 24-36 cookies.

5 cups sugar
2 cups honey
3/4 cup butter
1 cup lemon juice
3 eggs
3 egg yolks

5 pounds flour
1 cup baking powder
1 T. each ginger, cinnamon, and cloves
1 t. each nutmeg and salt
cardboard and tape

Combine sugar, honey, and butter and cook over medium heat until the butter melts. Add lemon juice, eggs, egg yolks. Stir in flour, baking powder, spices, and salt. Stir until the dough is mixed but still lumpy. On a floured surface knead with floured hands until the dough forms a smooth ball. Cover.

Build a cardboard house for the foundation. Cut four 7 x 10-inch pieces of cardboard (two for the side walls and two for the roof) and two 7 x 11-inch pieces for the ends of the house. Mark off 7 inches on each 11-inch side end panel for shaping the pointed gable. Then cut from this mark to the center of the top of the cardboard. Tape the cardboard sides together with masking tape and attach the roof. Place the house on a cardboard foundation and tape the two pieces together. Roll out a piece of dough on a floured surface until it is 1/2-inch thick. Cut dough the same size as the cardboard pieces. Bake the dough on a greased cookie sheet in a 350 degree oven for 30-35 minutes or until dough is browned. Cut remaining dough into chimney pieces and extra cookies cut from cookie cutters.

For the chimney, cut a 1 x 2-inch piece of dough, a 1 x 1 1/2-inch piece of dough, and two 1 x 2-inch pieces of dough with diagonal cuts on the short ends so the chimney will fit the roof slope. Bake these pieces and cookies made from leftover dough 20-25 minutes. When cool, spread a thin layer of frosting on the cardboard and press gingerbread pieces in place. Use frosting to attach candy to the house. Candy trim can include gumdrops, red hots, flower lollipops, M&M's, and chocolate bars.

Frosting:

3 egg whites   1 pound sifted powdered sugar

Beat egg whites with powdered sugar until mixture holds its shape. Keep frosting bowl covered with a damp cloth when not in use so the frosting doesn't dry out.

Simple Individual Gingerbread Houses

Remove the folded top and first 2 inches of a clean half-gallon paper milk carton with scissors. Cut down 4 inches in each corner crease, folding to the inside two opposing flaps. Bring remaining flaps toward each other and tape where they meet at the top. You now have foundation for house.

Using recipe above, mix frosting and cover the foundation with a thin layer. Cover with graham crackers. With extra icing, "glue" on pieces of assorted candy (M&M's, gumdrops, mints, chocolate chips, red hots, etc.) to decorate.

Windows and doors can be represented with squares of chocolate bars or long pieces of licorice. The chimney can be formed with a junior-size Milky Way bar with an upside down "V" cut into the end for roof placement.

ICING IDEAS
Cream Cheese Icing
A child's favorite!

3 ounces cream cheese
1 1/2 cup powdered sugar
4 T. butter or margarine
1 t. vanilla

Mix well together with electric mixer until light and fluffy. Spread on cake or cookies.

Chocolate Chip Frosting
While cake is hot, sprinkle with semi-sweet or milk chocolate chips. Let stand several minutes until chips are soft. Spread carefully over cake with knife or spatula.

FRUIT FIX-UPS
Easy-to-Eat Caramel Apples
Slice apples and put into individual bowls. Melt 1 package (14 ounces) caramel candies with 1/4 cup evaporated milk and pour over apple slices. Serve with spoons.

Banana Bobs
Peel bananas and cut in half crosswise; insert popsicle stick into cut end. Freeze, then dip into:

1. Honey thinned with warm water, then roll in granola. Return to freezer. Or,
2. Melted chocolate chips, then roll in chopped nuts or crispy rice cereal. Return to freezer.

Porcupines
Give each child half of an apple, toothpicks, and small cubes of cold cuts, cheese, cherry tomatoes, raisins, grapes, etc. Child can put chosen bits on toothpicks and stick into apple. All sorts of creations emerge!

Fruit Kabobs
Purchase bamboo skewers and a variety of fresh fruits—pineapple, strawberries, grapes, cherries, apples, oranges, watermelon, cantaloupe—whatever is in season and available. Slice the larger fruits into cubes or balls about one inch around. Invite children to fill their skewers with different pieces of fruit and then eat a piece at a time. (Be careful that younger children do not stick the skewers into their mouths!)

Grilled Cinnamon Apples
Quarter and core four apples. Place on a large sheet of heavy duty foil and sprinkle with 1 cup of red hot candies and 2 tablespoons butter. Seal foil around apples and lay over smoldering fire in grill 30 minutes.

SNACK STUFF
G.O.R.P. (Good Old Raisins and Peanuts)

Mix together choice of raisins, peanuts, M&M's, marshmallows, granola, candy corn, Cheerios, pretzels, sunflower seeds, chocolate chips, or any dry cereal. Healthy snack that can be put into small plastic bags for snack time!

Roasted Pumpkin Seeds

Great activity for children after pumpkin carving at Halloween!

Rinse fresh pumpkin seeds and spread on a cookie sheet. Add a little vegetable oil. Stir to coat seeds and then sprinkle with salt. Roast in 300 degree oven for about 30 minutes or until they are golden brown and crispy.

Finger Jello

Mix 1 1/4 packets of unflavored gelatin with 1/4 cup water and set aside. Mix 5/8 cup water and 1 (3-ounce) package fruit-flavored gelatin in a saucepan and bring to a boil. Add the original mixture and additional 1/4 cup water. Stir and pour into cake pan. Let cool for about 10 minutes. Put in refrigerator to chill. It really can be eaten finger-style! Make several colors and cut with cookie cutters.

LUNCH AND SUPPER IDEAS
Make-Your-Own-Pizza

Children can decorate a portion of a large pizza with toppings of their choice. An easy recipe for pizza dough follows. Alternatives to pizza dough are English muffin halves or flattened refrigerated biscuits.

Homemade Pizza Dough

1 1/2 cups flour
1 t. garlic salt
1 t. pepper
1 package yeast
1/2 cup warm water
1 t. sugar
1/4 cup salad oil

Mix flour, pepper, and garlic salt in a bowl. Soften yeast in water with sugar; add oil. Combine with flour and mix well. Cover with towel; let rise in warm place 30 minutes. Spread on greased pizza pan or cookie sheet.

Coat bread or dough with bottled pizza sauce and let children decorate with such toppings as sausage, hamburger, hot dog slices, pepperoni, grated mozzarella cheese, cheddar cheese, olives, onions, or green pepper. Bake at 425 degrees until cheese is melted and bread is golden, about 15 minutes.

Make-Your-Own-Submarines

Slice Italian bread rolls and offer children choice of following:

ham, salami, and other cold cuts
assorted cheese slices
lettuce
pickles, olives, onions
tomato slices
mustard, mayonnaise, ketchup

Let children create submarine as desired. Encourage them to be adventurous! Children could also create together one giant submarine with a large loaf of Italian bread sliced lengthwise. After sandwich is built, individual slices can be held together with fancy toothpicks. (Four-foot-long bread loaves are often available from a neighborhood delicatessen.)

Kabobs

Offer chunks of the following ingredients to children to fill skewers for kabobs:

sausage slices or links
hot dog slices
marinated steak bits
green pepper pieces
cherry tomatoes
pineapple chunks
canned new potatoes
olives

Children can create own kabobs and heat over grill or fire. (Make sure this is supervised!) Skewers might be dangerous for the very young child.

Walking Salads

Bugs-on-a-Log

Cut celery stalks into 4-inch lengths and fill with peanut butter. Press raisins into peanut butter here and there for "bugs."

Red Ants on a Log

Fill 4-inch celery pieces with cream cheese or favorite cheese spread. Sprinkle with paprika.

Dinner under Wraps

Wrap bologna slice around a pickle or long piece of cheese. Wrap bologna with cabbage or lettuce leaf and secure with toothpick.

Mini-Kabobs

Place cubes of cheese or meat, pineapple chunks, olives, pickles, etc. Stick on a toothpick.

BEST EVER BEVERAGES

Orange Frost

6 ounces orange juice concentrate
1/4-1/2 cup sugar
1 cup milk
1/2 cup water
1 t. vanilla
10 ice cubes

Blend in blender 10 seconds and pour into small glasses or cups.

Snow Cones

Make ice cubes from orange juice or lemonade. Crush cubes in blender to make a fruit slush.

Or try crushing regular ice cubes in blender with 1/2 cup water. Pour into glasses and add 2 tablespoons fruit juice concentrate (orange juice, grape juice, cranberry juice, etc.)

Make-Your-Own-Shake

Offer choice of following plus a blender to mix a marvelous new taste sensation!

Step One—Choose a liquid from:
   milk
   juices (orange, grape, pineapple, fruit punch)

Step Two—Add a thickener such as:

ice cream, sherbet, honey, yogurt, syrup, egg, pudding, malt powder, or cottage cheese

Step Three—Add a fruit such as:

strawberries, bananas, pineapple, fruit cocktail, peaches, or cherries

Make sure there is enough liquid!

CRAFT RECIPES

Playdough

Playing with playdough is a great activity for young children. You might also send it home in plastic baggies as a favor.

Mix: 1 5/8 cups flour

Boil: 1 1/2 cups water
      2 T. alum
      1/2 cup salt
      2 T. salad oil
      food coloring

Pour boiling mixture into dry mixture, stirring constantly. Knead with wooden spoons until cool enough to knead with hands. Keep sealed in plastic bag or plastic container.

Salt Dough

Use to make Christmas dough ornaments as an activity with the children or to send home as favors.

1 cup salt
2 cups flour
3/4 cup water
2 T. salad oil

Mix thoroughly. Store in airtight container. After modeling, bake in a 350 degree oven until object is lightly browned. Can be painted with acrylic paints when cooled.

When you are still interested in hosting your party at home—but not too sure as to how to entertain the children—check some of the following sources in your city.

The first stop is always the Yellow Pages of your phone book. Listings such as *Entertainers, Entertainment Bureaus,* and *Party Planning Services* will often give you some good names to call. Make sure you receive references from any of these groups before you contract with them to entertain at your celebration.

For plenty of audience participation, check with the **theater department** of local colleges and universities for students who might have a mime troupe. Also, area **children's theaters** might have a touring caravan or listing of those who do magic or storytelling, mime or creative dramatics. **Libraries** may also be helpful in locating children's storytellers.

Often **PTAs and preschools** have listings of entertainers that they use for their functions. These are great sources because they have already been tested and given a stamp of approval.

Many **service organizations** have clowns that perform for a small fee. Retired senior citizens and Shrine groups seem to have many such performing troupes as well as the American Red Cross Clown Corps.

Magic shops have a good lead on who in town does magic shows. And **puppet companies** can usually put you on to some performers who might free-lance.

Contacting **local art groups** for artists who do caricature and silhouette portraits serves as great entertainment plus is a party favor for the whole family to enjoy. Artists who create balloon sculptures are popular with little ones.

Zoos or nature centers sometimes have traveling wildlife programs presented by staff or volunteers.

ENTERTAINERS

Allow plenty of time in scheduling your event. Always, the best resource is to talk to your friends and to the parents of your children's friends. Word of mouth is often the only way to discover those little known treasures who perform just once in awhile—and just for fun. Sign them up immediately!

Record local entertainers and phone numbers here:

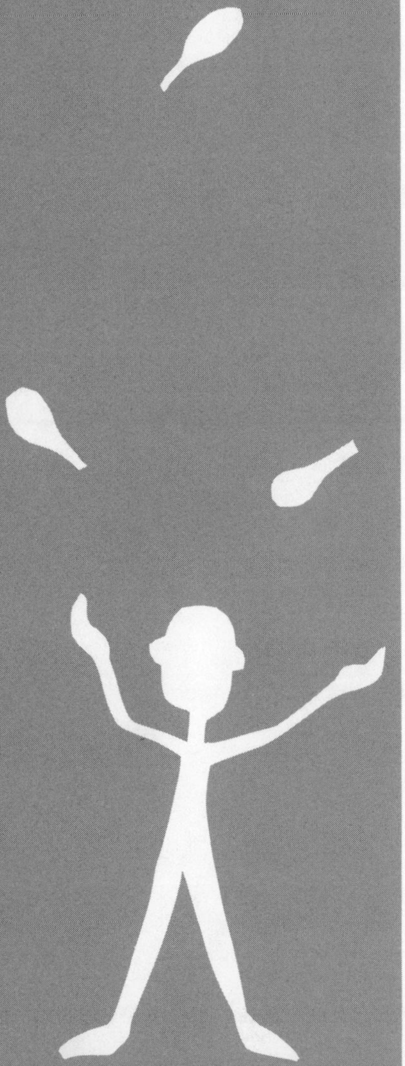

_____

_____

_____

_____

_____

_____

_____

_____

_____

_____

_____

_____

_____

_____

_____

_____

_____

_____

_____

_____

_____

_____

_____

If you don't feel up to having the children in your home—or just want to try something different—check into a center which specializes in giving kids a good time. Don't overlook obvious places such as a neighborhood park—remember it's just being together that makes up 90 percent of the fun!

Look through the entertainment section of your local newspaper or city magazines on a regular basis for upcoming events, festivals, openings, etc. As you read or hear of a review or item about some sort of entertainer or place to go with kids, note it in the space provided (when appropriate with event dates) after a listing in this section. Your records will be the envy of all your friends.

The following listing should turn up many ideas:

AMUSEMENT/THEME PARKS—offer a full day of fun for a group.
Notes:

_____

_____

_____

ART CENTERS—give hands-on experiences and something to take home.
Notes:

_____

_____

_____

ART GALLERIES—have special tours and exhibits just for children.
Notes:

_____

_____

_____

BOWLING ALLEYS—most have a party plan which includes two games, shoe rentals, snack, and sometimes ice cream and cake.
Notes:

_____

_____

_____

PLACES TO GO

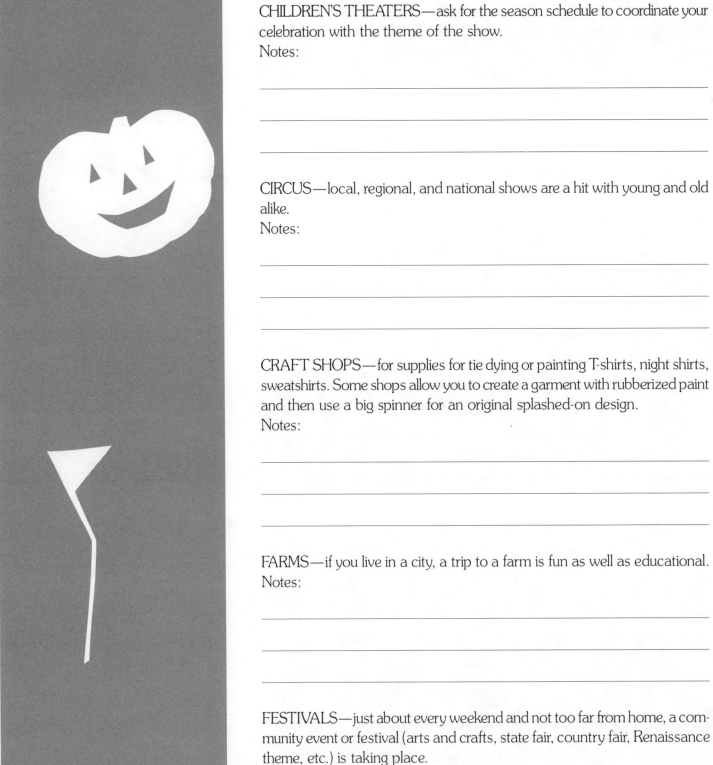

CHILDREN'S THEATERS—ask for the season schedule to coordinate your celebration with the theme of the show.
Notes:

_____

_____

_____

CIRCUS—local, regional, and national shows are a hit with young and old alike.
Notes:

_____

_____

_____

CRAFT SHOPS—for supplies for tie dying or painting T-shirts, night shirts, sweatshirts. Some shops allow you to create a garment with rubberized paint and then use a big spinner for an original splashed-on design.
Notes:

_____

_____

_____

FARMS—if you live in a city, a trip to a farm is fun as well as educational.
Notes:

_____

_____

_____

FESTIVALS—just about every weekend and not too far from home, a community event or festival (arts and crafts, state fair, country fair, Renaissance theme, etc.) is taking place.
Notes:

_____

_____

_____

FISHING—some areas allow free weekends where a license is not needed. A cookout would also be fun to do.
Notes:

_____

_____

_____

FIRE and POLICE DEPARTMENTS—tours with safety tips are usually provided for small groups.
Notes:

_____

_____

_____

FRISBIE COURSES—sometimes with miniature golf courses, have party packages.
Notes:

_____

_____

_____

GAME CENTERS—include pocket billiards, video games, pinball, etc.
Notes:

_____

_____

_____

HOT AIR BALLOONING—some locales offer rates based on increments of 30 minutes.
Notes:

_____

_____

_____

INDOOR SPORTS MALLS—many offer lock-in programs for larger groups. Overnight, children can enjoy soccer, indoor softball and batting cages, disco

area, video film room, video games, volleyball, golf, touch football, basket-ball, billiards, frisbee, in a supervised safe environment.
Notes:

_____

_____

_____

ICE SHOWS—touring companies try to make it to your area at least once a year.
Notes:

_____

_____

_____

INDUSTRY TOURS—local industries such as soft drinks, chip or candy manufacturers, bakeries, newspaper printing plants try to accommodate groups if given enough time.
Notes:

_____

_____

_____

MINIATURE GOLF COURSES—most party packages include 1½ hours of miniature golf, indoor or outdoor party tables, prizes and tournaments, cake and soft drinks.
Notes:

_____

_____

_____

MINI-CAR RACE TRACKS—kids love to have their pictures taken for their very own driver's license!
Notes:

_____

_____

_____

MOTELS WITH INDOOR POOLS—some motels will allow use of their pools for groups during certain hours upon rental of a room. You will need to check with each individually.
Notes:

_____

_____

_____

MOVIE THEATERS—always check times and listings because weekday times may not be the same as weekend times and you avoid having to reschedule a party.
Notes:

_____

_____

_____

MUSEUMS—natural history, science and technology, historical, children's, etc. normally have special events for kids.
Notes:

_____

_____

_____

ORCHARDS—picking fruit off the tree is a clever way to teach botany.
Notes:

_____

_____

_____

OBSERVATORIES AND PLANETARIUMS—exploring the galaxy makes for an interesting afternoon. Most have shows that change every few months—so call for schedule.
Notes:

_____

_____

_____

PARKS—some have special activities on the weekend featuring games and events as well as bike and hike trails.
Notes:

_____

_____

_____

PERFORMING ARTS EVENTS—professional theater, children's theater, puppet shows, ballet companies, symphonies, sometime allow tours backstage with a look at costume, make-up, and scenery areas.
Notes:

_____

_____

_____

PUMPKIN PATCHES—great place to take a group of children in the fall.
Notes:

_____

_____

_____

RADIO STATION TOUR—get a favorite disc jockey to show the kids the ropes of radio.
Notes:

_____

_____

_____

RIVERBOAT CRUISES—music, snack bars, and scenery will keep the kids busy.
Notes:

_____

_____

_____

RODEOS—excitement for all ages with a western theme for the party!
Notes:

_____

_____

_____

SKATEBOARD PARKS—most have pools and ramps for all levels of experience.
Notes:

_____

_____

_____

SKATING RINKS, ICE AND ROLLER—most skating rinks have a special plan for parties—usually a set fee for the first twelve children with an additional charge for each skater after that (includes skate rental, admission, drinks, etc.).
Notes:

_____

_____

_____

SOUND RECORDING BOOTHS—individuals or groups can record their vocal performances using the studio's background tracks.
Notes:

_____

_____

_____

SPORTS STADIUM TOURS—or see a game (don't forget university tournaments).
Notes:

_____

_____

_____

STABLES—horseback riding, bonfires, hayrides are fun for older children.
Notes:

_____

_____

_____

TRAIN RIDES—in certain areas of the country, Amtrak has short train runs.
Be certain to check the schedule.
Notes:

_____

_____

_____

TROLLEY RIDES—many cities now have trolleys for public transportation
that can also be rented for celebrations.
Notes:

_____

_____

_____

TV SHOWS—your town may have a children's show where guests may sit
in the audience or participate in (such as Romper Room).
Notes:

_____

_____

_____

TV STUDIO TOUR—most stations are equipped to provide tours and a
background look at the electronic media.
Notes:

_____

_____

_____

WATER SLIDE PARKS—if you're not near the ocean this will make up for it.
Notes:

_____

_____

_____

WILDLIFE RESERVES—allow you to see nature at its best without going too far out of your way.
Notes:

_____

_____

_____

ZOOS—and don't forget petting zoos for little ones.
Notes:

_____

_____

_____

PARTY PROVISIONS

Finding balloons and crepe paper is not usually difficult—but sometimes finding unique party supplies can be a challenge. The Yellow Pages listings below should put you on to some fun decorations, favors and party props:

BALLOON BOUQUETS
Notes:

_____

_____

_____

CARD AND GIFT SHOPS
Notes:

_____

_____

_____

CARNIVAL SUPPLIES
Notes:

_____

_____

_____

CRAFT STORES
Notes:

_____

_____

_____

HELIUM—Check "welding supplies" or "helium"
Notes:

_____

_____

_____

LIBRARIES (for videos)
Notes:

_____

_____

_____

PARTY SUPPLIES—also Discount Paper Goods
Notes:

_____

_____

_____

TEACHER SUPPLY STORES
Notes:

_____

_____

_____

SINGING TELEGRAMS
Notes:

_____

_____

_____

TOY STORES—have Balloon Sculpture Kits and Bubble Hoop Sets
Notes:

_____

_____

_____

Your own city probably has many special restaurants that are notorious for providing a good time. Think about some of the following ideas for additional spots.

CANDY STORES—might offer candy-making classes
Notes:

_____

_____

_____

COOKIE BAKERIES—find one that makes special celebration cookies or cookies on a stick
Notes:

_____

_____

_____

DELIS—see if they make 5-foot long sandwiches
Notes:

_____

_____

_____

50's DINER—or any restaurant with a theme for a party
Notes:

_____

_____

_____

HAMBURGER CHAINS—most have party packages and a party room
Notes:

_____

_____

_____

PIZZERIAS—often have special parties and sometimes tours
Notes:

_____

_____

_____

POPCORN FACTORIES—often give tours and samples
Notes:

_____

_____

_____

THERE ARE REASONS TO CELEBRATE IN:

ALABAMA at NASA Space Station Tours in Huntsville; **ALASKA** at Fairbanks Riverboat Discovery; **ARIZONA** at Pima Air Museum; **ARKANSAS** at Diamond Cave, Ozarks National Forest; **CALIFORNIA** at Hearst Castle Tour; **COLORADO** at Ute Indian Museum; **CONNECTICUT** at Mystic Seaport Museum with the Tall Ships; **DELAWARE** at the Cape May-Lewes Ferry Mini-cruise; **FLORIDA** at Monkey Jungle in Miami; **GEORGIA** at Okefenokee National Wildlife Refuge; **IDAHO** at Ghost Town, Idaho City; **HAWAII** at the Sugar Train Ride on Maui; **ILLINOIS** at the Lincoln Park Zoo; **INDIANA** at Indianapolis Motor Speedway Museum; **IOWA** at the Amana Colonies; **KANSAS** at Wichita's Old Cowtown Museum; **KENTUCKY** at Kentucky Derby Museum; **LOUISIANA** at Avery Island Jungle Gardens & Bird Sanctuary; **MAINE** at Boothbay Railway Museum; **MARYLAND** at Baltimore's National Aquarium; **MASSACHUSETTS** at Old Sturbridge Village; **MICHIGAN** at Detroit Children's Museum; **MINNESOTA** at Brainerd's Paul Bunyon Amusement Center; **MISSISSIPPI** at Petrified Forest near Jackson; **MISSOURI** at Hannibal, the home of Mark Twain and Tom Sawyer; **MONTANA** at Custer Battlefield National Park; **NEBRASKA** at Minden's Pioneer Village; **NEVADA** at Hoover Dam; **NEW HAMPSHIRE** at Shaker Village; **NEW JERSEY** at Great Adventure Safari and Entertainment Park; **NEW MEXICO** at Taos Pueblos; **NEW YORK** at Storytown U.S.A.; **NORTH CAROLINA** at USS North Carolina Battleship Memorial; **NORTH DAKOTA** at Theodore Roosevelt's National Park; **OHIO** at Cleveland's Sea World; **OKLAHOMA** at the National Cowboy Hall of Fame; **OREGON** at Oregon Wildlife Fish Hatchery; **PENNSYLVANIA** at Hershey's Chocolate World Tour; **RHODE ISLAND** at Newport's Tennis Hall of Fame; **SOUTH CAROLINA** at Charleston's Spoleto Festival; **SOUTH DAKOTA** at Mount Rushmore; **TENNESSEE** at Lookout Mountain Incline Railway; **TEXAS** at Dallas' Southfork Ranch; **UTAH** at Hansen Planetarium in Salt Lake City; **VERMONT** at Sugar Bush Valley Ski Area; **VIRGINIA** at Jamestown Festival Park; **WASHINGTON** at Indian Rock Paintings: **WEST VIRGINIA** at Exhibition Mine; **WISCONSIN** at The Dells; and **WYOMING** at Cody's Buffalo Bill Historical Center.

NOTE ANY SPECIAL CELEBRATIONS (WITH DATES) IN YOUR AREA:

_____

_____

_____

_____

_____

_____

_____

_____

_____

_____

About The Authors

Carol Cowden and Patsy Shawver are both busy working mothers who collected ideas and resources while planning their children's parties. Thus, they created *Celebrate!*

Carol, the mother of John and Jenny, has lived in Kansas City eighteen years. She has an education degree from the University of Missouri, has taught French and preschool, and for the past ten years has been the director of the children's ministry at a local Presbyterian church.

Patsy, mother of Erin and Brian, is a native Kansas Citian. Her degree in elementary education is from the University of Kansas. She has worked as assistant volunteer coordinator at a creative art workshop for children and is currently the Community Relations Coordinator at the Salvation Army.

ORDER DIRECT
CALL 816-756-1490

☐ **YES,** I want _____ copies of
CELEBRATE! Parties for Kids (national)
for **$9.95** each plus $2 shipping.

☐ **YES,** I want _____ copies of
CELEBRATE! Parties for Kansas City Kids
(includes resource section—names,
addresses, phone numbers—for KC
Metro area) for **$9.95** each plus
$2 shipping.

Method of Payment

☐ Check to:

Westport Publishers
4050 Pennsylvania Ave.
Kansas City, MO 64111
for $ _____ .

☐ Charge my credit card

☐ VISA   ☐ MasterCard

ACCT. # _____

EXP. DATE _____

SIGNATURE _____

Ship to: _____

_____

_____

_____

_____

- -

ORDER DIRECT
CALL 816-756-1490

☐ **YES,** I want _____ copies of
CELEBRATE! Parties for Kids (national)
for **$9.95** each plus $2 shipping.

☐ **YES,** I want _____ copies of
CELEBRATE! Parties for Kansas City Kids
(includes resource section—names,
addresses, phone numbers—for KC
Metro area) for **$9.95** each plus
$2 shipping.

Method of Payment

☐ Check to:

Westport Publishers
4050 Pennsylvania Ave.
Kansas City, MO 64111
for $ _____ .

☐ Charge my credit card

☐ VISA   ☐ MasterCard

ACCT. # _____

EXP. DATE _____

SIGNATURE _____

Ship to: _____

_____

_____

_____

_____